WRITING RESEARCH PAPERS

A Student Guide
for Use with
Opposing Viewpoints®

by Andrew Harnack, Ph. D.

Greenhaven Press, Inc.
P.O. Box 289009
San Diego, CA 92198-9009

Library of Congress Cataloging-in-Publication Data

Harnack, Andrew, 1937–
    Writing research papers : a student guide for use with opposing viewpoints / by Andrew Harnack.
        p.   cm.
    Includes bibliographical references (p.) and index.
    ISBN 1-56510-099-9 : (acid-free paper)
    1. Report writing—Handbooks, manuals, etc.   2. Research--Handbooks, manuals, etc.   I.   Title.
LB2369.H32   1994
808'.02—dc20
                                                            93-4317
                                                            CIP

Contents

A Preface
for Students

Writing Research Papers, a guide for students working with Opposing Viewpoints books, is designed to help college students develop their own thinking and to write and report what they have learned to others. Written to help students think critically, develop documentation skills, and write for college or university audiences, this guide can be used with any book in the Opposing Viewpoints series. As a guide for writing research papers, it provides students with a general introduction to the language and methods of colleges and universities.

As a tool for writing, Opposing Viewpoints books are ideal. Because each one of the topics in the Opposing Viewpoints series is controversial, the books allow students to hone the critical thinking and reading skills necessary to write a thoughtful and complex essay. By distinguishing fact from opinion, students will measure the strength of various arguments and eventually find out where they stand on an issue. Then, having taken a position, students will try, in writing, to persuade others to agree with their arguments.

When college students work on a topic—frequently in the very act of writing—they discover that they undergo a shift in opinion or conviction. As students work through this guide and an Opposing Viewpoints book, they, too, may change their minds about an issue, perhaps even taking points of view opposite ones held earlier, perhaps modifying their original positions considerably. If that happens, students are encouraged to change their minds about an issue and reflect upon that change in writing.

This guide has many important features that will help the student:

- an introduction to the resources available in every Opposing Viewpoints book
- an emphasis on critical reading so that students learn how to construct meaning from significant articles or essays
- assignments that match the topic under discussion and encourage students to acquire knowledge of their research topic while they develop research and documentation skills
- a student essay that demonstrates how a research paper is written (Appendix A)
- evaluation guides that can be used by individual writers, peers, and instructors (Appendix B)
- suggestions for a portfolio presentation that records students' writing processes and gives them opportunities to reflect on what they have learned (Appendix C)

Writing Research Papers is itself written much like a research paper. Thus, as college writers read and study this book, they will notice that it follows the Modern Language Association (MLA) style of documentation. This allows readers to see exactly how this documentation style is used in a piece of writing.

In writing research papers, students will write multiple drafts of various parts: introduction, thesis, background section, lines of argument, refutation of opposing points of view, conclusion, and a bibliography of works cited. Thus, although students work on only a single project, they compose and recompose parts of that project and, by degrees, shape it into a presentation copy. Writing Research Papers was developed and used successfully in classrooms with thousands of students. I hope that the book will be equally as successful for thousands more.

—Andrew Harnack

To the Instructor

As a writing instructor using *Writing Research Papers*, you will find this text valuable for many reasons. It promotes critical reading and thinking, demonstrates use of the MLA style of documentation, and offers suggestions for developing effective student research, discussions on argumentation styles, advice for revising and editing, and suggestions for portfolio presentation of papers. In addition, the twenty-four suggested writing assignments are keyed to evaluation guides that may be used in previewing, reviewing, and assessing student writing.

As the author of this text, I know that professional writing instructors must translate the best of composition theory into effective classroom practice. To that end, this book was written; and as my mentors I list Edward P.J. Corbett, Andrea Lunsford, Ann E. Berthoff, Peter Elbow, Pat Belanoff, Robert Conners, and Richard W. Paul, among others. I have always found that effective teaching works best in the company of such colleagues.

I now count you as a colleague. If you have not already received the *Instructor's Guide for Writing Research Papers*, contact Greenhaven Press for your copy. Because I have always leaned heavily on the advice of those who share theoretical insights and provide practical suggestions on how best to teach reading and writing to students, I invite you to join the teaching community of those of us who use this text. By sending me your e-mail address, you will be linked to an electronic network (*WRP Webwork*) that will periodically provide you with communiqués, announcements, and teaching suggestions.

As you work with *Writing Research Papers*, I wish you every success and hope to hear from you. If you and your students have success with this text, tell me. If I can be of help to you professionally, drop me a line or send a message via e-mail. I would be delighted to hear from you.

Andrew Harnack
Department of English
Eastern Kentucky University
Richmond, KY 40475

e-mail address: ENGHARNACK@ACS.EKU.EDU

1

Reading Critically

All books in the Opposing Viewpoints series have been carefully designed to present a spectrum of views on a given issue. Many of the essays are written by experts in their field and were originally published in distinguished journals of opinion, books, government reports or documents, or by special interest organizations.

The contents of each Opposing Viewpoints book are divided generally into five chapters, and each chapter contains four to six essays. Individual chapter titles often pose a question that is answered by the viewpoints. For example, *Racism in America: Opposing Viewpoints* is subdivided into five narrower subtopics posed as questions. This method of organization provides students with a valuable model. It shows how a broad topic can be broken down into several subtopics, each one worthy of serious study. This narrowing is advantageous because you do not have to spend valuable time trying to break down a large topic into more focused and manageable areas of investigation.

In each chapter of each Opposing Viewpoints book, pairs of opposing essays debate even more narrowly focused issues. Each chapter contains four to eight paired essays that create a running debate. Each viewpoint is preceded by a short quotation that best expresses the author's main argument. This format quickly places readers into the middle of a controversial issue and helps them recognize how one view opposes another. Each book may contain as many as fifteen possible topics to investigate, research, and write about.

All of the essays in each Opposing Viewpoints text introduce arguments. Reading these essays is simply the first step in entering an area of controversy. For this reason, periodical bibliographies are placed at the end of each chapter to lead you to the second step of research—reading as much as you can about a topic. In addition, each book contains a book bibliography that lists other important resources, many of which are available in your college or university library. Each Opposing Viewpoints text also contains a list of organizations to contact that can be used to proceed to yet another step into research. The design of each Opposing Viewpoints text reinforces the idea that research in your topic, as in all areas of research at a college or university, is a multileveled and expanding process.

Understanding and Grasping the Issues

The first step in writing a research essay is to learn to take careful notes on what you read. For most people, note taking is a difficult process. When they go back to their notes, they discover that they simply jotted down some "factoids," scratched out some ideas, and made a few sketchy notes about ideas. These notes turn out to be not very helpful. Because most students are novices at research, they need several good methods for digging into their topic's world of ideas and information.

Assuming that you know little about the issue you wish to investigate, you have only one option: you must familiarize yourself with as much relevant information as you can. Generally speaking, the more you know about your topic, the better you are able to write. As a researcher, therefore, one of the first things you need to do is quickly develop an overall understanding of your topic. As soon as possible, you must dive into the world of ideas, facts, information, opinions, and arguments that make your topic interesting, perhaps even fascinating. While many books have been written about how to start getting involved in research, one of the best ways is to start reading and taking notes at the same time. You need to be able to answer these questions:

- What happened?
- Who is involved in the issue?
- How did things develop to where they are now?
- What are the major questions?
- What are the options?
- What is at stake?
- Generally speaking, how are people arguing?
- What do we know for sure?
- What statistical information do we have?

When looking for answers to questions like these, simply gather information, data, and facts.

THREE READING AND WRITING STRATEGIES

One of the most effective ways to gather answers to such questions—and thus have command of the basic facts—is to read all of the essays in the specific chapter of the Opposing Viewpoint book that deals with your subtopic. While reading, think about what you're reading, and make notes by completing a rhetorical précis, taking dialectical notes, or doing charted readings. These options, which will be explained in the following pages, will help you to produce extensive and complete notes. After doing this reading and writing, you will likely decide which side of an argument you wish to pursue in your essay because you will have informed yourself of the argumentative options.

Strategy 1: The Rhetorical Précis

Writing a *rhetorical précis* is an effective and popular strategy for understanding an article's point of view. It was first advocated by educator Margaret K. Woodworth in 1988. Practice in writing a rhetorical précis forces you to read with greater attention and to write with control and conviction. It helps you convey to other people ideas that you have read about.

The rhetorical précis, as Woodworth defines it, is a *highly structured, four-sentence paragraph* that records the essential rhetorical elements of a unit of writing. It includes the name of the writer, the content, the major assertion, the mode of development or support, the stated or apparent purpose, and the relationship established between the writer and the audience. Each of the four sentences requires specific information. As you write the rhetorical précis, you are encouraged to use brief quotations to convey a sense of style and tone. Once you have mastered the form, you will find that the technique will enable you to understand and evaluate what others are saying and writing.

The rhetorical précis will help you assess the credibility of your sources and evaluate new information in relation to what you already believe. Moreover, practice in the form will help you review the strategies of the author, examine the form of the discourse, discover the author's purpose or hidden agenda, and be aware of the nature of the audience for whom something is written. Simply lifting information and paraphrasing it as trustworthy is potentially dangerous because it perpetuates the myth that all printed information is equally reliable, accurate, and useful. That's not true. Writers package their information to suit their needs. As researchers, you need to examine a writer's package: the wrapping, the manufacturer, the contents, and to whom the package is addressed.

The summaries you will write using the rhetorical précis will also answer the basic *who, what, where, when, how, why,* and *to whom* about a piece of writing. In addition to summarizing content, a rhetorical précis analyzes the circumstances leading up to and informing a piece of writing. It clarifies how someone else chose to say something, in a particular way, for some purpose, to certain other people.

The Rhetorical Précis

1. Name of author and title of work (publishing information, date, and page numbers in parentheses); a rhetorically accurate verb (such as *asserts, argues, suggests, believes, reports);* and a "that" clause containing the major assertion (thesis statement) of the work.
2. A brief but accurate explanation of how the author develops or supports the thesis, usually in the same order as was developed in the essay.
3. A statement of the author's apparent purpose, followed by an "in order to" phrase.
4. A description of the intended audience.

Here is a rhetorical précis written by a student who, working on the topic of animal rights, had narrowed her focus to questions about justifying the use of animals in scientific experimentation. It is a good example of a well written précis because it provides an accurate but brief summary of an article. Notice how it fulfills the requirement that a rhetorical précis be written in *four* sentences:

Jane Goodall in "Primate Research Is Inhumane" (Animal Rights: Opposing Viewpoints. Ed. Janelle Rohr. San Diego, CA: Greenhaven, 1989: 95–100) argues that most laboratories using primates engage in inhumane practices. She supports her argument through detailed descriptions of lab environments and draws special attention to the neglect of psychological comforts which these primates endure until they sometimes become insane. Her purpose is to speak on behalf of the chimpanzees (because they cannot speak for themselves) in order to persuade her readers to see that if we do not fight for improvements in lab care, "we make a mockery of the whole concept of justice." Goodall writes to those who have compassion for other species and who might have enough courage to speak out for chimpanzees and other primates.

Many students find the first sentence of the rhetorical précis the most difficult sentence to compose. One difficulty in constructing this sentence is that students tend to use general words such as *writes* and *states* to indicate what the author is doing. To overcome this difficulty, you need to find a verb that genuinely describes what your author does in the essay. Here is an example:

> Frederick A. King, in "Primate Research Is Humane" (Animal Rights: Opposing Viewpoints. Ed. Janelle Rohr. San Diego, CA: Greenhaven, 1989: 90–94), **argues** that . . . .

Other verbs that may accurately describe what the author is doing are *insists, suggests, contends, believes, asserts, reports,* and *indicates,* among many others.

A second difficulty involves the "that" clause, which is designed to demand a complete statement that emphatically announces the essay's thesis. Students often like to use *about* and *how* and thus avoid stating the thesis: that is, "Tom Regan . . . writes about the animal rights movement" or "Peter Singer . . . states how he feels about the environmental crisis. . . ." Neither of these introductions allows you to say what Regan or Singer actually claims to be true about animals and people. By forcing yourself to use the word *that,* you obligate yourself to restate the central idea of the essay.

In sentence 2 you tell your reader what happened, section by section, in the essay. Do not simply highlight one or two ideas; instead, you must show how the author supported the main idea by paraphrasing major arguments, restating important information—or whatever it was that the author did to support the controlling idea of the essay. Because sentence 2 may contain several ideas, it may be helpful to link several independent clauses with one or more semicolons. Here is an example of such a second sentence in a rhetorical précis that joins what otherwise might be several self-standing independent clauses:

> King supports his contention by asserting that "the rules for conduct of research, procedures, and standards" at most primate centers ensure that primates receive humane treatment; for example, at the Yerkes Regional Primate Research Center all research proposals are reviewed and monitored so that they "not only meet but exceed current U.S. Public Health Service regulations"; special animal care teams daily visit all apes and monkeys "so that any health problem can be detected and treated early"; whenever invasive surgical procedures are used, "veterinarians and scientists alike use the same anesthetics and sterile procedures followed in human hospitals."

This sentence, quite long by ordinary standards, contains three smaller sentences, each one of which is joined to another by a semicolon. By using this strategy, you can manage to compose a rhetorical précis within the prescribed limit of four sentences.

In sentence 3, as Woodworth suggests, you state the author's purpose, using an "in order to" phrase to make sure the purpose is actually stated. Woodworth explains why:

> [In the third sentence, students] sometimes inadvertently restate the thesis: "The author's purpose is to prove that. . . ." It helps to remind students that one purpose is always to put forward a thesis, but there are others as well. The "in order to" phrase keeps students from falling back on "Her purpose is to inform" and requires that they look beyond to assess what the author wanted the audience to do or to feel as a result of reading the work. (159)

Including the "in order to" phrase thus forces you to state the author's reason for writing. Compare the following two sentences and notice, for example, how the use of the "in order to" phrase in the second sentence makes the rhetorical analysis more complete:

> King writes so that he can explain how primates are treated humanely.

> King writes in order to assure his audience that they can trust researchers to engage in justifiable primate research.

Including the "in order to" phrase in sentence 3 requires that you search out and articulate the real intention of an author.

In sentence 4 you indicate for what audience the author has written the essay. It's important to realize that most writers target specific audiences and then deliberately set about to influence their thinking. Only naive readers assume that authors write articles for everyone. By targeting audiences, writers give themselves more control over the flow of their information and ideas. Once you see an author's intended audience, then you can look for the strategies used to influence and shape the readers' response. Take, for example, King's essay. It was originally written and delivered as a paper for an audience of professional psychologists. Addressing fellow scientists and researchers, King frequently reminds them that, from his point of view, "the question of the value of research with primates is a crucial one." Indeed, he concludes his essay with a plea to his colleagues—his specific audience:

> It is now up to us to inform the public about what we are doing and why it is essential to continue our work, or suffer the consequences of unwarranted, but unanswered attacks on our purposes, practices, and achievements.

Because King's message is directed toward his professional colleagues, he can establish a relationship characterized by reassurance, mutual commitment to research, and a concern for the future. Realizing this, you could write sentence 4 like this:

> As a researcher himself, King urges his colleagues to "inform the public" that such research is humane.

With this last sentence, the four-sentence rhetorical précis is complete. It presents the author's main idea, the supporting arguments and evidence, the purpose for writing, and an audience analysis; together the four sentences provide a complete rhetorical précis:

> Frederick A. King, in "Primate Research Is Humane" (Animal Rights: Opposing Viewpoints. Ed. Janelle Rohr. San Diego, CA: Greenhaven, 1989: 90–94), argues that primates used in experimental research are treated humanely. King supports his contention by asserting that "the rules for conduct of research, procedures, and standards" at most primate centers ensure that primates receive humane treatment; for example, at the Yerkes Regional Primate Center all research proposals are reviewed and monitored so that they "not only meet but exceed current U.S. Public Health Service regulations"; special animal care teams daily visit all apes and monkeys "so that any health problem can be detected and treated early"; whenever invasive surgical procedures are used, "veterinarians and scientists alike use the same anesthetics and sterile procedures followed in human hospitals." King writes in order to assure his audience that they can trust researchers to engage in justifiable primate research. As a researcher himself, King urges his colleagues to "inform the public" that such research is humane.

Should the need arise, the information this rhetorical précis contains can effectively be used in a research paper.

✏ **Suggested Writing Assignment 1** ✏

Write a Rhetorical Précis on One or More Essays in Your Opposing Viewpoints Text
Attach the Evaluation Guide

Choose one or more articles in your text that you think will help you understand your area of research. Read the essays carefully and write a four-sentence précis on each article. Follow the model.

Strategy 2: Dialectical Note Taking

Often when we read, we dip into a text for information, find something interesting, and then proceed to forget most of what we've read. We don't bother to think about it. Often we don't even take the time to wrestle with the text to see what it really says. We skim through ideas we already know and skip over material that is difficult or challenging. For some purposes, such "speed reading" is okay. But for college- or university-level classes, we often need to read carefully and slowly. We need to struggle with articles and books to grow and develop intellectually. Dialectical note taking is a special and highly effective way of combining reading and writing. The word *dialectical* comes from two Greek words: *dia* meaning "through" and *lektos* meaning "spoken." Anything that is dialectical, therefore, is something that is "spoken through"—that is, thoroughly discussed. The method of dialectical note taking, first proposed by educator Ann E. Berthoff of the University of Massachusetts, helps you learn effectively and think critically.

Dialectical note taking will help you avoid being a relaxed reader by forcing you to overcome the tendency to skim over a text. Before you read, number in sequence each paragraph of a section, essay, or chapter that you intend to read. Next, get one or more sheets of paper and divide them into two columns: title the left column Observations-Notes; title the right column Responses. As you read each paragraph, make notes about its content in the left column. Jot down what you observe to be important in the paragraph by briefly rephrasing or paraphrasing it. When making this paraphrase, you can use abbreviations; you don't have to write in sentences. You can also make lists and create informal outlines. Whether you write in sentences or use some other method, it is important that you rephrase the paragraph's main ideas in some helpful fashion.

After you have made your initial notes or observations in the left column, the next thing to do is think about what you have noted. To do this, in your right column make a comment on what you've written in the left column.

An example on page 9 shows how one student read and thought about the first two paragraphs of Jay Stuller's "Human Needs Are More Important than Animal Rights" from *Animal Rights: Opposing Viewpoints*.

As you can see, this student made a *double-entry analysis* of his material. And when he made his dialectical notes, he observed what he might otherwise have missed. He read the text and got basic and important ideas from observing the text. But equally important, this student also thought about what he observed. He connected his reading to his

Observations-Notes	Responses
Par. 1 Humans, especially those in Western cultures, have traditionally ranked the interests of men, women, and children higher than the interests of wildlife and stock animals.	I think this assertion is true. I wonder, however, why Stuller qualifies it by saying this ranking is true of "Western cultures generally." Do Eastern cultures think differently? If so, why?
Par. 2 If faced with the choice between starving and eating deer, we will, of course, bar-b-que "Bambi."	This too is true. But I don't think our culture would ever call such food a "Bambiburger." I don't think so. We most often disguise the meat we eat by giving it some other name other than the animal's name. Why?

observations about life. He noted that Western cultures have developed a hierarchical understanding of animal life and wondered if an Eastern perspective might be different. He also agreed that, when confronting starvation, humans would readily eat deer. But he also noted that we don't often label meat products by the animal's names. He asked himself, "Why?"

Such critical reading and thinking is important when researching a controversial topic. It helps you formulate the strengths and weaknesses of arguments. When the time comes for you to state your own thinking in the form of a thesis, you will already have done some critical thinking on what may become your own sustained argument in a research paper. You will have developed both an understanding of what others say and how you react to their arguments.

Suggested Writing Assignment 2

Make Dialectical Notes on One or More Essays in Your Opposing Viewpoints Text
Attach the Evaluation Guide

Choose one or more articles that you think will help you understand your area of research. Number the paragraphs, prepare sheets for dialectical note taking, read paragraph by paragraph, and make dialectical note entries. Follow the model.

Strategy 3: Charted Readings

Doing a charted reading of an essay is another effective strategy for critically reading essays of the length of those typically included in the Opposing Viewpoints series. Using this technique guarantees that you will successfully follow an essay's lines of argument, paragraph by paragraph. You will more thoroughly understand how the author arrives at his or her conclusion.

To chart a reading, work with each paragraph in the essay sequentially. Next, using a large sheet of paper (8½" × 11" turned horizontally works well), create enough boxed spaces to chart what you are reading, one box for each paragraph. Number each box. Then, within each box, summarize as best you can the main ideas developed in each paragraph. Use whatever system of abbreviations and shorthand note taking that works for you. Draw diagrams and idea maps if they are helpful. Below,

| 1. It's often difficult to understand a new idea like the notion that nonhuman animals have rights. | 2. One reason for not understanding why an animal can be said to have rights is that animals are radically different from us. | 3. We tend to think of animals as objects. Our specialized vocabulary (A lab rat is a "resource tool") distances us from understanding that "nonhuman animals as creatures, like ourselves, experience pain and suffering and have complicated emotional lives." | 4. We know we wouldn't do to people what we do to animals. We understand our right not to be eaten or experimented on. What we don't know is that these rights are not ours exclusively. Only a certain arbitrariness excludes animals from having such rights. |

for example, is how one student charted Spence Carlsen's "Human Needs Are Not More Important than Animal Rights" taken from *Animal Rights: Opposing Viewpoints.*

As can be seen from this example of a charted reading, not every detail contained in every paragraph is included. You simply showcase the main ideas. The result is an abbreviated display of the whole essay. This valuable technique allows you to see an entire medium-sized essay on one page. Such miniaturization has several advantages. You trace, paragraph by paragraph, the unfolding message or argument to see exactly how an idea is developed. You can also note how much attention is given to any one point. Seeing everything at once allows you to perceive the essay's construction and reveals strategies for structuring your own writing. It will certainly make you keenly aware of what a text says and how it presents an argument.

5. We make up reasons to explain our rights over animals. Some use their religion as justification; others see animals as just machines. But our rights are really based on power. We're stronger than they are. Animals just can't stop us. In the past stronger humans have also denied rights to weaker humans.

6. We keep animals in labs because we have the power to cage them and do what we want to with them. "The extent of experimentation is limited by imagination, not law."

7. We put animals on our plates because there too we are more powerful. We breed, raise, hunt, trap, club, shoot, and harpoon them because we've got the power.

8. Once we see the system for what it is, then we can take "the first step toward understanding the meaning of animals' rights." Such rights belong to human and non-human animals alike. The next step is to follow our conscience and do something to help animals.

> ## Suggested Writing Assignment 3
>
> **Make a Charted Reading of One or More Essays
> in Your Opposing Viewpoints Text**
> *Attach the Evaluation Guide*
>
> Choose one or more articles that you think will help you under-
> stand your area of research. Number the paragraphs, prepare
> sheets for charted reading, read each paragraph carefully, and
> chart the entire essay.

ORGANIZATIONS TO CONTACT

Each Opposing Viewpoints text contains a list of organizations to contact.
These organizations—many of which are professional, public relations
institutions advocating particular points of view—are important sources
of information. Although the list of organizations to contact is discussed
further in Chapter 4, when you will work on expanding your research, it
is a good idea to examine the list early and contact those who can send
you information, because it sometimes takes several weeks for individual
organizations to respond. Those that are relevant to your area of research
should, therefore, be written to and contacted as soon as possible. Indeed,
early in the semester, a small investment of time and the cost of several
stamps can pay off handsomely later on when important research information arrives by mail. Take time, therefore, to write several organizations that can provide you with significant resources. Notice that a brief
description of each organization follows its name and address. Select several that appear to be for a given position in your area of research and
several that appear to be against. Using the sample letter provided at the
end of this chapter, you may compose an appropriate letter requesting
information.

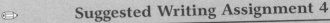

Suggested Writing Assignment 4

Write to Several Organizations for Information
Attach the Evaluation Guide

One excellent way to begin research is to write several organizations and request information. If you are working with a group of writers on the same research topic, you might ask individual members to write to different organizations and share the information received. Ask each writer to make a copy of his or her letters before they are mailed; hand those copies in for your instructor to review.

Sample of Letter to an Organization

Telford Hall Box #497
Eastern Kentucky University Campus
Richmond, KY 40475

September 2, 1994

American Association for Laboratory Animal Science
70 Timer Creek Drive, Suite 5
Cordova, TN 38018

Dear AALAS:

As a student at Eastern Kentucky University, I am doing research on the topic of animals' rights. I am especially interested in receiving information from various points of view. Please send me whatever information you publish on the rights of animals. Thank you for your time and information.

Sincerely,

Mary Graves

Mary Graves

cc: Mrs. Linda Doerge, Instructor

2

Preparing a Background Report

It is quite possible, even likely, that students know little about the research topic they are going to investigate and write about. For some students, this realization produces anxiety, resulting in writer's block. Afraid that their lack of knowledge may prove embarrassing later on, they have misgivings about their ability to write well under such circumstances. For such students, the idea of doing research may be intimidating. It may conjure up images of students sitting woefully at their desks, bleary-eyed, kept awake by coffee, buried deep in stacks of books, worried if they'll ever get their papers done. Unfortunately for some students, the stereotypical images may be true; from past experience they know little about the process of research and thus tend to postpone or even bypass it as much as possible. Other students, unduly panicked by the whole thought of doing research, may resort to ordering ready-made papers advertised and sold by outfits that cater to helping students pass off such work as their own. Doing research devolves into simply a matter of buying a product. But writing a research paper need not be exhausting or intimidating if you understand the process and take advantage of knowing how research is actually done—and done well.

To help demystify the research process, Andrea Lunsford and Robert Connors wrote a popular writing handbook that provides a helpful definition of the word *research*:

> The English word *research* derives not only from the French *chercher*, which means "search," but also from the Late Latin *circare*, which means "circle around, explore." Research, then, is a way of exploring a subject by circling carefully around and around it, a process that the editors of the eleventh edition of the *Encyclopedia Britannica* identify as all "investigations . . . based on sources of knowledge." Without

research, they go on, "no authoritative works could have been written, no scientific discoveries or inventions made, no theories of any value propounded." (525)

Research involves learning how to investigate a topic from many angles. By "circling around" a topic, the researcher probes different viewpoints and perspectives to develop a whole picture. Such probing—whether in the research lab or in the library—often results in one's becoming an expert in a field of study. In the end, it's this sense of expertise that ultimately gives researchers and their writing a solid, authoritative voice.

You should, therefore, expect that most research—especially the sort that circles around a topic—is more or less fairly messy in the beginning. Because researchers often step into unknown territory, they may at first feel confused and lost. Yet, if at this point, the temptation to postpone pushing ahead can be avoided, most students will break through their discomfort to become effective researchers.

WHERE TO START WRITING

When starting to write a research paper, you must first be able to communicate basic information about a topic. You need to answer the following questions for yourself before you begin to write:

- What are the critical terms and ideas that should be clearly defined?
- What are the problems involved?
- What statistics and reports clarify the topic?
- Who is involved?
- What have others said about the topic?
- What is the historical context?
- What changes have occurred?
- What will happen if no solutions are found?
- What analogies can be created to describe the problem?
- What solutions have been proposed?

By finding answers to such questions and sharing them with readers, you give yourself and others a foundation upon which to build further discussion. In short, you first write about background information to educate yourself about a research topic.

While you are writing the background section for your research paper, you will, of course, continue to research your topic. You will also learn how to use the Modern Language Association (MLA) style of documentation (Chapter 3), how to expand your research (Chapter 4), and how to take research notes (Chapter 5). After you are well informed about your topic—by writing the background section—you will then be in a position to create a thesis, structure the rest of your paper (Chapter 6), and state your view with an effective presentation (Chapter 7).

This background information will become an important part of your research paper. When it appears in your paper, it provides your readers with an overall picture to help them see your point of view. Think of your background information, therefore, as an aerial photograph or a large map that will provide a broad picture for your more detailed analysis and arguments—your own thesis.

This initial project—writing the background section—should continue for several weeks. While writing, incorporate outside sources to demonstrate that you are learning how to use the MLA style of parenthetical citation.

OPTIONS FOR DEVELOPMENT

Listed below are options that you may use in various combinations to provide sufficient coverage for your topic. These options reflect how we think about and understand a vast range of subjects. Responding to these suggestions can help you view your topic from many angles. Not all will be productive, but at least a few should open up new possibilities.

Define One or More Important Terms

What critical terms related to your topic should be clearly understood by your intended audience? This question leads to definition. You may want to include a well developed paragraph (or set of paragraphs) that accurately defines a critically important idea, term, or word. For example, suppose you have decided to write on the rights of animals in biomedical research. It would be important to provide a working definition of the phrase *biomedical research* so that no one confuses it with biophysical, biosocial, or biotechnical research.

To help your readers understand significant concepts, make a list of key words, ideas, phrases, or terms that often appear in the discussions on your topic. Look over your list and pick one or more that will genuinely contribute to your readers' understanding of your topic. These are the terms you will want to define in your background information.

The larger definitions we are concerned about cannot be found in dictionaries; indeed, at the very least they exceed those provided by dictionaries. Thus you will not want to define something by simply saying,

"According to *Webster,* biomedical research is. . . ." That kind of definition is only for early evening television quiz shows and not very helpful. Delija J. Valiukenas, in *Writing with Authority,* describes more helpful definitions:

> The only definitions that a reader wants to see on the printed page are usually either those that aren't in most dictionaries; those that comment on, criticize, or disagree with the dictionary; or those that have little to do with the dictionary meaning. (150)

Although Valiukenas's statement is perhaps too strongly worded, her suggestion has a lot of merit. Readers want definitions that help them understand something new. They want you to provide them with a larger vision. It's your job, therefore, to provide them with definitions that expand their thinking.

There are many ways of defining an idea or term. One effective way is to create a formal definition consisting of three parts: term, class, and distinguishing characteristics. For example, both medical researchers and animal rights activists would agree that the following definition of animal research is an accurate one:

The Term, Phrase, or Concept	The Class to Which It Belongs	The Distinguishing Characteristics
Animal research is	experimentation	that employs the use of • live, • dead, • or anesthetized animals to study the effect of • chemical substances, • surgical procedures, • or diseases of animals

Notice that this formal definition is based upon a concise, logical pattern that provides a maximum amount of information in a minimum amount of space. You create such definitions in four steps. First, give the term to be defined; second, use a verb like *is* (or *means,* or *may be defined as*); third, put your term into its proper class (what next in the order of things it belongs to); and fourth, give all of its peculiar distinguishing characteristics (all the things that are peculiar only to what you're defining). Usually you write such a formal definition in one sentence.

A formal definition sets you well on the way to writing a paragraph or set of paragraphs. In effect, you write a topic sentence that controls the development of your paragraphs. Take the animal research example above. Most likely your next sentences will develop the notion of its being an experiment. In doing this, you might describe what laboratories look like, who works in them, and what sort of animals are experimented upon. The sentences that follow would explain what sort of live, dead, or anesthetized animals are used. You might provide some statistics or classify the animals. You might give a famous example of one such lab—perhaps one that has used baboons to study head injuries, as described by Peter Singer in *Animal Liberation* (81). After some examples, no doubt, perhaps you would proceed to clarify what you mean by *chemical substances, surgical procedures,* and *diseases.* All told, you might have eight to ten sentences that provide your readers with an extended definition of animal research. In the process, you have enlarged their understanding, their vision, and their thinking.

Suggested Writing Assignment 5

Develop Background Information

Use the MLA Documentation Style
Attach the Evaluation Guide

Compose one or more paragraphs within which you use a formal definition; include the term, the class, and the distinguishing characteristics. Explain each of the characteristics adequately. When using outside sources, see Chapter 3 for documentation style guidelines.

Use Comparisons, Contrasts, or Analogies

Another way to explain a word or idea is to make a comparison, contrast, or analogy. In the following example, freshman writer Vicky Alabassi compares a chicken broiler shed to a prison:

> A broiler shed for chickens, like a prison for humans, is not an attractive place to live. But unlike prisons, which are expensive to maintain and which by law can not be overcrowded, broiler sheds are a cheap way to farm chickens and are always overcrowded.

Elsewhere in the paper, she paraphrases Peter Singer's explanation of speciesism in *Animal Liberation,* which also employs the use of comparison:

Singer believes that speciesism is like racism and sexism in that one group allows the interests of its own members to override the greater interests of members of another group; thus one race believes itself superior to another, one sex thinks itself better than another, or one species thinks itself more privileged than others. (9)

Comparison emphasizes the *similarities* among things while contrast points out the *differences*. An analogy, usually an extended comparison, helps to make understandable something that is unfamiliar by comparing it to something familiar. As an analogy, for example, the process of electrical conduction might be likened to water flowing in a stream. When making comparisons, contrasts, or drawing analogies, do not overextend them tediously.

✏️ **Suggested Writing Assignment 6** ✏️
_____

Develop Background Information

Use the MLA Documentation Style
Attach the Evaluation Guide

Compose one or more paragraphs within which you create comparisons, contrasts, or analogies to help your reader better understand an idea that might otherwise remain unclear. When using outside sources, see Chapter 3 for documentation style guidelines.

Describe a Process

Readers often need to follow an action to understand its significance. In a process analysis, you explain how something is accomplished or how it happens. Here, for example, is how Jean Bethke Elshtain, Centennial Professor at Vanderbilt University, in "Why Worry About the Animals?" (*The Progressive*, March 1990) describes one test frequently given to animals:

For years, industry has determined the toxicity of floor wax and detergents by injecting various substances into the stomachs of beagles, rabbits, and calves, producing vomiting, convulsions, respiratory illness, and paralysis. The so-called LD-50 (lethal dose) test ends only when half the animals in a test group have died. No anesthesia or pain killers are administered.

By showing how something works, you give readers dynamic images by which they can see an activity or function.

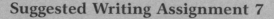

Suggested Writing Assignment 7

Develop Background Information

Use the MLA Documentation Style
Attach the Evaluation Guide

Compose one or more paragraphs within which you describe one or more processes important to an understanding of your topic. When using outside sources, see Chapter 3 for documentation style guidelines.

Provide Examples

You can clarify an idea by providing examples. Examples are particularly useful when you need to support generalizations or bring abstractions to life. Peter Singer in *Animal Liberation,* for example, wishing to emphasize that people do, in fact, change their thinking and attitudes about animal experimentation, provides this example:

> More dramatic still was the change of heart shown by the Canadian philosopher Michael Allen Fox. In 1986 the publication of his book *The Case for Animal Experimentation* seemed sure to earn him a prominent spot at scholarly conferences as the chief philosophical defender of the animal research industry. The drug companies and lobbyists for animal experiments who thought they had, at last, a tame philosopher they could use to defend themselves against ethical criticism must have been dismayed, however, when Fox suddenly disavowed his own book. In a response to a highly critical review in *The Scientist,* Fox wrote a letter to the editor saying that he agreed with the reviewer: he had come to see that the arguments of his book were mistaken, and it was not possible to justify animal experimentation on ethical grounds. Later Fox followed through on his courageous change of mind by becoming a vegetarian. (242–243)

Just as a picture is sometimes worth a thousand words, a well chosen example can help your readers visualize and remember a generalization or argument you wish to make.

Suggested Writing Assignment 8

Develop Background Information

Use the MLA Documentation Style
Attach the Evaluation Guide

Compose one or more paragraphs within which you support important generalizations with representative examples or illustrations to make such generalizations convincing or credible. When using outside sources, see Chapter 3 for documentation style guidelines.

Review the Origins of a Word

When confronted with unfamiliar words, readers often appreciate an explanation of the origins of unfamiliar words. You can, therefore, often clarify an idea by analyzing its etymology, that is, the root meaning of a word. Because the word *vivisection* was an important term in her research paper, Katisha Seward provided this explanation:

> The word <u>vivisection</u> comes from the Latin words <u>vivus</u> (meaning "alive") and <u>sectio</u> (meaning "a cutting"). Vivisection, therefore, is the act of cutting into or dissecting the body of a living animal.

When you refer to a word as a word in a sentence, you underline the word to which you are referring.

Suggested Writing Assignment 9

Develop Background Information

Use the MLA Documentation Style
Attach the Evaluation Guide

Compose one or more paragraphs within which you explain the meaning of an important word by reviewing its origins. When using outside sources, see Chapter 3 for documentation style guidelines.

Use What Others Have Said

Frequently you can reinforce an observation or an argument by using an apt quotation. Here, for example, Harold J. Morowitz, in "Christianity Does Not Support Animal Welfare" (*Animal Rights: Opposing Viewpoints*), contends that the influence of Aristotle continues to be felt among scientists. He helps his argument by introducing a quotation written by a leading nineteenth-century physiologist:

> The extension of the Aristotelian perspective into the age of science is seen most forcefully in the writings of Claude Bernard. In his book *Experimental Medicine* (1865), he addressed the issue of animal use and gave what I believe is still the scientist's justification for work on higher mammals:
>
> > Have we the right to make experiments on animals and vivisect them? As for me, I think we have the right, wholly and absolutely. . . . No hesitation is possible; the science of life can be established only through experiment, and we can save living beings from death only after sacrificing others. Experiments must be made either on man or on animals. Now I think that physicians have already made too many dangerous experiments on man, before carefully studying them on animals. I do not admit that it is moral to try more or less dangerous or active remedies on patients in hospitals, without first experimenting with them on dogs. . . . It is essentially moral to make experiments on an animal even though painful and dangerous to him, if they may be useful to man. (102)

By citing a recognized authority such as Bernard, Morowitz adds strength to his presentation. As this passage illustrates, a citation of an expert should always refer the reader to the source, here indicated by the page number in parentheses "(102)." Such a citation is generally accompanied by a reference to the expert's credentials.

◦⟹   **Suggested Writing Assignment 10**   ⟸◦

Develop Background Information

Use the MLA Documentation Style
Attach the Evaluation Guide

Compose one or more paragraphs within which you support and buttress your own writing with the ideas of others. When using outside sources, see Chapter 3 for documentation style guidelines.

Place Your Issue in a Historical Context

You can often help your readers better understand a research topic with a brief historical narrative. In a preliminary draft, one student, Jane Hagness, traced the history of attitudes toward animal experimentation:

> Humans have experimented on animals for centuries. And, as might be expected, philosophers, theologians, and scientists have justified and condemned such activity from a variety of perspectives. Especially since the Renaissance, as Gerald Carson reminds us, with the birth of scientific study, it is not surprising that "animal experiments, neglected in the Middle Ages, were revived" to provide "the basis for the science of comparative anatomy and a more precise knowledge of the physiology of the nervous system" (23). In 1627, responding to this renewed use of animals as research subjects, the English statesman Francis Bacon suggested that animals might as well be used to test the safety of certain products. In the same century the French philosopher René Descartes contended in a letter to Henry More (5 Feb. 1649) that as "thoughtless brutes" animals are actually God-created machines (*automatons*) whose body parts work like the gears of clocks. Because clocks feel no pain when taken apart, Descartes said, neither do animals. Other philosophers disagreed. Voltaire, for example, in his *Philosophical Dictionary* retorted: "Answer me, machinist, has nature arranged all the spring of sentiment in this animal that he should feel no pain?" The romantic Jean-Jacques Rousseau also objected by saying that animals share sensibility with humans: "They ought to partake of natural right; so that mankind is subjected to a kind of obligation even toward the brutes" (41).

By providing the reader with an understanding as to how opposing viewpoints have developed, this student allowed her audience to appreciate the complexity of an issue and to more fully observe the spectrum of ideas.

✏️   **Suggested Writing Assignment 11**   ✐

Develop Background Information

Use the MLA Documentation Style
Attach the Evaluation Guide

Compose one or more paragraphs within which you write a brief historical review to help your readers understand the present situation regarding your topic. When using outside sources, see Chapter 3 for documentation style guidelines.

Make a List of Events, People, or Things

You can help your readers understand the depth of an issue, the extent of a problem, the magnitude of a concern, or the direction of a movement by simply giving them a list of items. One student writer, for example, quoting philosophy professor Sidney Gendin, provided this list when he wanted to show how animals are routinely used to test the toxicity of many household products:

> The following products are regularly tested on animals: insecticides, pesticides, antifreeze, brake fluids, bleaches, Christmas tree sprays, silver and brass polish, oven cleaners, deodorants, skin fresheners, bubble baths, freckle creams, eye makeup, crayons, inks, suntan lotions, nail polish, zipper lubricants, paints, food dyes, chemical solvents, and floor cleaners. (Animal Rights and Human Obligations, 187–199).

Clearly such a list supports the generalization that the use of animals in experimentation is far-reaching and helps readers judge for themselves its extent.

☞   **Suggested Writing Assignment 12**

Develop Background Information

Use the MLA Documentation Style
Attach the Evaluation Guide

Compose one or more paragraphs within which you provide a list to show the extent of something in your topic. When using outside sources, see Chapter 3 for documentation style guidelines.

Divide an Issue into Smaller Parts

Dividing is an action that breaks a unit into parts. By dividing something, you put things, ideas, or people into groups to help your reader perceive the relationships and differences among them more clearly. By way of illustration, observe how student Ricardo Tejedo demonstrated that members within animal rights organizations tend to divide themselves into two groups:

> Concerned and informed people who are convinced they need to do something to help animals generally fall into two groups: the "reformers" and the "abolitionists." Reformers, on the one hand, think of themselves

as policy changers, working, for example, toward reforming a system which inhumanely uses animals in labs, or toward creating better protective legislation for animals. They frequently support medical groups like Physicians for the Ethical Treatment of Animals and participate in demonstrations expressing outrage at needless and objectionable experiments. On the other hand, the abolitionists propose more radical solutions. They contend that we must immediately and completely call a halt to all experimentation on animals. Animals, abolitionists often argue, possess everything necessary to really be "somebody" and not just "some thing." They have emotional lives, have preferences and make choices, organize their lives into meaningful patterns, care for their young, engage in thinking, anticipate the future, have and use memories—in short, they can celebrate life. Simply because such animals cannot express their emotions and thoughts in our language does not give us the right to subject them to suffering and pain. We must stop using them as objects in experiments.

Such a division helps readers see where the dividing line falls between two philosophies. If the unit to be divided is separated into three or more groups, it is important not to forget someone or something important.

✏️   **Suggested Writing Assignment 13**   ✏️

Develop Background Information

Use the MLA Documentation Style
Attach the Evaluation Guide

Compose one or more paragraphs within which you separate an issue into smaller parts so that both the whole and the individual parts can be more easily seen and analyzed. When using outside sources, see Chapter 3 for documentation style guidelines.

Classify Ideas, Issues, or Objects

Classifying is a form of dividing. By classifying, you put things, ideas, events, or people into categories to help readers perceive relationships in new ways. When you classify, you apply a classifying principle to separate units and place them in appropriate subclasses. By way of illustration, observe how the following paragraph classifies the many groups that maintain different views on animal experimentation. The classifying principle—the *appropriateness* of animal experimentation—is consistently applied:

> There is a wide variety of views regarding the appropriateness of using animals in research. Many organizations, like the American Medical Association (AMA), believe that it is entirely appropriate to conduct experiments on animals in order to advance both human and animal well-being. Thus researchers like C. Cohen and Dennis M. Feeney argue that the use of animal subjects in research should be encouraged rather than discouraged. Researchers with more moderate views than those of the AMA, such as M. Fox, are less sure that we need to increase the use of animals in research. They argue that no animals should be used unless it is apparent that a clear medical benefit is to be realized from the experiment. Still others are less committed to experimentation involving animals; the Physicians Committee for Animal Care (PCAC) and Psychologists for the Ethical Treatment of Animals, for example, believe that we should drastically reduce our research on animals by developing effective alternatives. Finally, antivivisectionists, such as Roy Kupsinel, contend that no animal should be used in any painful procedure in order to make human life more comfortable. Obviously with such divergent convictions, it is not easy to determine who is right.

By classifying, you let your readers see an orderly arrangement of what might be perceived as a confusing mass of information.

✎   **Suggested Writing Assignment 14**   ✐

Develop Background Information

Use the MLA Documentation Style
Attach the Evaluation Guide

Compose one or more paragraphs within which you place a range of ideas, issues, or objects into subclasses so that your readers see an informative display of such ideas, issues, or things. When using outside sources, see Chapter 3 for documentation style guidelines.

Provide Statistical Information

Readers appreciate statistics, especially when provided comparatively, because they give a feel for the dimensions of an issue or problem. For her readers, one student provided this information:

Although exact figures are difficult to obtain, and estimates as to numbers of animals used in research vary greatly, the total number of animals used throughout the world each year in research is very large. According to Senator Orrin Hatch, the Office of Technology Assessment estimates that in the United States between 17 and 22 million animals are used in research each year:

> Approximately 10% of laboratory animals are cats, dogs, hamsters, guinea pigs, rabbits, and nonhuman primates such as chimps and monkeys; 15% are birds, reptiles, fish, and amphibians; and about 75% are rats and mice. (59)

Tom Regan reports that approximately 250 million animals are used for a vast variety of scientific experiments each year throughout the world ("Illgotten," 22).

If you decide to provide charts and tables containing complex statistical information (or illustrations, maps, and so forth), follow, as research specialist L. Sue Baugh insists, two principles. First, make sure such visual presentations are "essential to your report and not used to conceal a lack of content." Be sure your illustrations "provide important information and not be used simply to fill out the page number requirements or to impress the instructor." Second, be certain your illustrations or charts support and clarify your text; do not allow them to replace it (*How to Write Term Papers and Reports* 156).

The *MLA Handbook*'s directions for placing any tables and illustrations into your text are straightforward and simple:

> Place illustrative material as close as possible to the part of the text that it illustrates. A table is usually labeled "Table," given an arabic numeral and captioned. Type both label and caption flush left on separate lines above the table and capitalize them as you would a title (do not use all capital letters). Give the source of the table and any notes immediately below the table. . . . Double-space throughout, making ruled lines as needed.
>
> Any other type of illustrative material—for example, a photograph, map, line drawing, graph, or chart—should be labeled "Figure" (usually abbreviated "Fig."), assigned an arabic numeral, and given a title or caption. . . . A label, title, or caption is ordinarily given directly below the illustration, flush with the left margin. (83–84)

Credit the source of all illustrative, statistical, and graphical material even if you yourself create the tables or graphs from data in another source.

☞   **Suggested Writing Assignment 15**   ☜

Develop Background Information

Use the MLA Documentation Style
Attach the Evaluation Guide

Compose one or more paragraphs within which you provide statistical information to give your readers an understanding of trends, demographics, and other significant data. When using outside sources, see Chapter 3 for documentation style guidelines.

Good writers usually do not limit themselves to using only one or two of the strategies presented in this chapter as they develop background information. Generally they combine several approaches so that together they can build up information from more than one perspective. As you work on your background section, examine the background section of the model paper in this guide.

☞   **Suggested Writing Assignment 16**   ☜

Write Your Background Section
Attach the Evaluation Guide

Combining material written for assignments 5 through 15 (and using any other additional writing), compose the background section of your research paper. This section will provide your readers with a context to help them understand an issue: its development, scope, critical terms, and whatever else elucidates the topic. In the background section, establish common ground, common understandings, which both you and your reader can agree upon. Give your reader a context for understanding whatever arguments and proposals you may later develop. Know what length your instructor expects this section to be. Background sections for student papers are usually at least three or more pages long. When using outside sources, see Chapter 3 for documentation style guidelines.

3

Using the MLA Documentation Style

One of the difficulties students encounter when they are learning to document their sources by using the MLA style is that they must learn to do several things at once. Like jugglers, students writing research papers are required to manipulate at least three balls almost simultaneously: a research ball, a writing ball, and a documentation ball. The complex nature of the task—learning how to juggle research, writing, documenting—makes the first attempts difficult and sometimes frustrating.

Many instructors help students solve this problem by introducing documentation as early as possible so that students have an opportunity to practice, learn from their difficulties, and eventually demonstrate a high level of competence by the end of the semester. If, for example, you are writing a background report as your first writing project, you may be given several weeks to compose it. During this time, you will read articles, pamphlets, encyclopedia entries, and chapters in books and record information from many sources. At the same time, you will compose early drafts of your text, building up paragraphs, arranging ideas, supporting a thesis. While all of this is going on, your instructor will begin telling you how to document your sources. By explaining the logic of a documentation technique, showing you models, and discussing the readability of a documented text, your instructor will progressively show you how to develop a mature and serviceable style. Responding to your instructor's comments (and perhaps peer evaluations), you will, in time, become competent in documentation.

The way researchers have documented their sources has changed dramatically in the past decades. At one time, it was common practice to include notes containing information about sources of information or other authors' ideas. These notes were called footnotes when placed at the foot, or bottom, of the page; when placed at the end of an article or chapter, they were called endnotes. Today, however, the extensive use of both footnotes and endnotes is not popular as it once was. When they are placed at the bottom of a page, they can become distracting; placed at the end of an article or book, they may be a nuisance to find. In place of extensive footnoting, therefore, many researchers prefer the use of *parenthetical citation*. When providing important information or ideas, researchers refer their readers to a source listed in *Works Cited* by placing the citation in parentheses immediately after the quote.

There are two major versions of this basic parenthetical citation style: that of the American Psychological Association (APA) and that of the Modern Language Association (MLA). Writers in disciplines such as psychology, sociology, and anthropology prefer the APA style, fully described in the *Publication Manual of the American Psychological Association*. Other disciplines have designed their own distinctive styles of documentation; thus, for example, researchers in mathematics use *A Manual for Authors of Mathematical Papers*, and those doing research in law employ *A Uniform System of Citation*.

This chapter shows you how to document sources by using the MLA style of parenthetical citation, a style often preferred by those who teach in the humanities, language arts, and other fields. Written by Joseph Gibaldi and Walter S. Achtert and published by the Modern Language Association (MLA) in 1988, the *MLA Handbook for Writers of Research Papers* is the bible for writers using the MLA style. It contains sound advice on the following important subjects:

- selecting topics
- compiling a working bibliography
- taking notes
- ways to avoid plagiarism
- how to do effective outlining
- language and style
- the mechanics of writing (spelling, punctuation, and so forth)
- the format of the research paper
- how to set up tables and illustrations
- preparing the list of works cited
- how to document sources

The *MLA Handbook*, available in almost all libraries and many bookstores, should be consulted if you come across a problem regarding documentation not discussed in this chapter.

Many English instructors use the MLA style when reporting their research and writing for publication. Consequently, they feel comfortable teaching it to their students. As you have noticed, this book—*Writing Research Papers*—uses the parenthetical documentation style when it documents the source of an idea, an exact quotation, or a particular piece of information.

The practice of citing references within the text and keying the citations to a list of works cited is easy to master, and you will come to appreciate the simplicity and efficiency of this procedure. In fact, you will discover that your own research writing style will improve because in-text citation facilitates the blending of quotations, paraphrases, and summaries with your text.

One of the best ways to see how the MLA style works is to read and study a research paper that uses parenthetical documentation. Appendix A contains such a paper by Sue Mattingly. Her paper "Does Animal Research Really Benefit Human Health?" demonstrates how most of the conventions are used.

Avoiding Plagiarism

The reason that researchers must learn to thoroughly document other works is to avoid plagiarism. Gibaldi and Achtert clarify the concept of plagiarism this way:

> Plagiarism is the act of using another person's ideas or expression in your writing without acknowledging the source. The word comes from the Latin word *plagiarius* ("kidnapper"), and Alexander Lindey defines it as "the false assumption of authorship: the wrongful act of taking the product of another person's mind and presenting it as your own" (*Plagiarism and Originality* [New York: Harper, 1952] 2). In short, to plagiarize is to give the impression that you have written or thought something that you have in fact borrowed from someone else. (21)

Plagiarism includes the presentation of material composed or revised by any person other than the student who submits it, as well as the deliberate falsification of references. Since your instructor will assume that material presented by you is indeed your own unless otherwise indicated, all quoted material must be in quotation marks, and all paraphrases, quotations, significant ideas, and organizations must be acknowledged by some form of documentation acceptable to your instructor.

Plagiarism is a form of academic dishonesty, and many colleges and universities consider it a serious offense. Because plagiarism is a serious violation of academic ethics, the penalties are often severe. Depending on the severity of the infraction, instructors may give a failing grade for a plagiarized assignment, they may notify departmental chairs and deans of the infraction, they may refer the student to a disciplinary board, or they may submit the case to a committee on academic practices with the recommendation that the student, if otherwise eligible, not be permitted to graduate with honors.

Of course, information commonly shared and already known by your audience does not have to be documented. Thus, for example, if you were writing about nuclear proliferation, the fact that the United States dropped the first atomic bomb on Hiroshima, Japan, on August 6, 1945, is common knowledge, available in many sources and mentioned by the media each year on that date. You would not be obliged to give credit to a source for this information. But once you begin to provide the details surrounding that event, such as information concerning the Manhattan Project and the first atomic explosion at Alamogordo, New Mexico, you would be obliged to cite your sources. As Michael E. Adelstein and Jean G. Pival in *The Writing Commitment* make clear, "Generally, everything in your research paper should be documented if it is not based on your own knowledge and if it is not common knowledge" (426). If you have any doubt about committing plagiarism, go ahead and cite your sources; then talk with your instructor about your concerns.

The Logic of the MLA Parenthetical Citation Style

The logic of the MLA style is simple. In the text of your paper, you provide a key signal—like the name of an author—which refers your reader to complete information about the source in a list of works cited. With the text and works cited list next to one another, as shown on page 33, you can see how the system of parenthetical citation works.

By examining the relationship between the text and the works cited list, you can see how the two work together. First, notice that the author provides an introductory name signal—in this instance the authors' names. With these names, the reader can locate the exact source in the alphabetized works cited listing. In other words, putting the names of Jasper and Nelkin in the sentence using their quotation guarantees that their names and complete information about their book will also appear in the alphabetized list of works cited. If readers want to examine the original source of this quotation, they can simply consult the list of works cited.

Second, notice that—in this instance—the author provides an exact quotation with beginning and ending quotation marks, indicating exactly what is being used, word-for-word, from the source.

Third, observe that the reader is given the exact page location of the quotation conveniently within parentheses "(115)" at the end of the citation. A period follows the parenthesis.

How Your Writing Keys Itself to the Works Cited Listing

A typical text page

Names of authors mentioned ──── The controversy over the rights of animals covers many areas of concern. But as James M. Jasper and Dorothy Nelkin make clear, ──── Signal verb

"the use of animals in scientific research is at once the most emotional and the most controversial, the most broadly publicized and the most widely criticized of all the issues raised by the animal rights movement" (115). ──── Page numbers of original source given in parentheses after the quotation, paraphrase, or summary

Vivisectionists (literally, those who believe in "cutting up" live animals for purposes of research) and antivivisectionists (those who oppose such sectioning) are in fundamental disagreement about the usefulness and morality of experimentation using animals.

A typical works cited listing

Alphabetized by last name ──── Jasper, James M., and Dorothy Nelkin. The Animal Rights Crusade: The Growth of a Moral Protest. New York: Free Press, 1992.

Periods mark off major segments and conclude entry

Readers thus have everything they need to successfully negotiate the text: a name as a key signal that refers them to an entry in the Works Cited, the quotation itself, and, in parentheses, the exact page number on which the quotation appears.

Because the list of works cited is the only place where your reader can locate complete and precise information about the sources you have cited, you must be careful to make your Works Cited thorough and accurate. Only when your works cited list is complete and accurate will your readers know exactly where they can find the sources of words, ideas, and evidence you have incorporated into your text.

Once you understand the logic of the parenthetical citation system, only two things remain to be learned to make it work for you and your readers:

1. You need to learn how to construct a listing of entries for your work cited page(s).
2. You need to practice composing sentences that have the signals (like the author's name) that will direct your readers to the works cited page for complete source information.

Although your list of works cited will appear at the end of your paper, Gibaldi and Achtert recommend that "you should *draft it in advance* [emphasis added], recording the works you plan to mention so that you will know what information to give in parenthetical references as you write" (86). This is exceptionally sound advice. By having your list of works cited already composed and ready for reference, you will more easily be able to find effective ways to key your sources to the works cited.

Creating the List of Works Cited

The following models for citations from books, articles, and other sources show you how to make entries for your list of works cited. While this list is not exhaustive, it does contain models for most of the sources that students use in research papers. Remember that the list of these models is a reference tool. When using such a list, it's best not to try to memorize the models. Simply refer to them often; in time you will internalize the models well enough to use many of them almost automatically. If you are ever in doubt about how to construct an entry, do not hesitate to consult your model. Always follow its form exactly.

Models for Books
A Book by a Single Author
Regan, Tom. The Case for Animal Rights. Berkeley, CA: U of California P, 1983.

Two or More Books by the Same Person
In citing two or more books by the same person, give the name in the first entry only. Thereafter, in place of the name, type three hyphens and a period and give the title. List the books alphabetically by title.

Rollin, B. E. Animal Rights and Human Morality. Buffalo, NY: Prometheus, 1981.
---. The Unheeded Cry: Animal Consciousness, Animal Pain and Science. New York: Oxford, 1989.

A Book by Two or More Persons
If there are more than three authors, you may name only the first and add *et al.* (Latin for "and others").

Mason, Jim, and Peter Singer. <u>Animal Factories</u>. New York: Harmony Books, 1990.
Balls, M., et al., eds. <u>Animals and Alternatives in Toxicity Testing</u>. London: Academic Press, 1983.

A Book by a Corporate Author
American Veterinary Medical Association. <u>Principles of Veterinary Medical Ethics</u>. Chicago: AVMA, 1973.

A Book with an Editor
Langley, Gill, ed. <u>Animal Experimentation: The Consensus Changes</u>. New York: Chapman and Hall, 1989.

An Anthology or Collection of Essays
Rohr, Janelle, ed. <u>Animal Rights: Opposing Viewpoints</u>. San Diego, CA: Greenhaven Press, 1989.
Swisher, Karin, and Tara P. Deal, eds. <u>The Elderly: Opposing Viewpoints</u>. San Diego, CA: Greenhaven, 1989.

An Individual Work in an Anthology or Collection of Essays
Millstone, Erik. "Methods and Practices of Animal Experimentation." <u>Animal Experimentation: The Consensus Changes</u>. Ed. Gill Langley. New York: Chapman and Hall, 1989.

An Introduction, Preface, Foreword, or Afterword
Langley, Gill. Preface. <u>Animal Experimentation: The Consensus Changes</u>. New York: Chapman and Hall, 1989.

Cross-References
Cross-referencing is especially helpful for students working with an Opposing Viewpoints text. To avoid unnecessarily repeating information when citing essays from the same collection, first list the anthology or collection itself with complete publication data. (See, for example, the model for an anthology or collection of essays.) Then cross-reference individual articles to that entry. When cross-referencing, state the author and title of the piece, the last name of the editor of the collection, and the relevant page numbers. Alphabetize all entries as usual.

Jablonski, David. "Endangered Species Should Be Saved." Rohr 139–42.
Rohr, Janelle, ed. <u>Animal Rights: Opposing Viewpoints</u>. San Diego, CA: Greenhaven, 1989.

A Multivolume Work
Inge, M. Thomas, Maurice Duke, and Jackson R. Bryer, eds. <u>Black American Writers: Bibliographical Essays</u>. 2 vols. New York: St. Martin's, 1978.

A Book in a Series
Tesar, Jenny. <u>Endangered Habitats</u>. Our Fragile Earth Ser. New York: Facts on File, 1992.

A Pamphlet
Treat a pamphlet as you would a book. If the pamphlet carries no date, indicate so by the abbreviation *n.d.* (meaning "no date").

Animal Legal Defense Fund. <u>Objecting to Dissection</u>. San Rafael, CA: n.d.

Physician's Committee for Responsible Medicine (PCRM). <u>The Facts About Animal Experimentation</u>. n.d.

Models for Articles
A Signed Article in a Reference Book
Walens, Stanley. "Animals." <u>The Encyclopedia of Religion</u>, 1986.

An Unsigned Article in a Reference Book
"Wildlife Refuges." <u>The Encyclopedia of Environmental Studies</u>, 1991.

An Article in a Journal with Continuous Pagination
Scholarly journals, sometimes appearing no more than four times a year, publish articles containing original research. Most often the page numbering continues without interruption from one issue to the next. Annually, such journals are assembled into bound volumes with continuous pagination. You may ignore the issue number and the month or season if the article you are citing appears in a journal that paginates continuously throughout the volume.

Horton, Larry. "The Enduring Animal Issue." <u>Journal of the National Cancer</u> Insti-tute 81 (1989): 736–43.

An Article in a Weekly Journal That Begins Pagination with Each New Issue
Karpati, Ron. "A Scientist: 'I Am the Enemy'." <u>Newsweek</u> 18 Dec. 1989: 31.

An Article from a Monthly or Bimonthly Periodical
When citing a periodical published every month or two months, simply give the month and year. Do not give the volume and issue numbers even if they are listed.

Goldberg, Alan M., and John M. Frazier. "Alternatives to Animals in Toxicity Testing." <u>Scientific American</u> Aug. 1989: 24–30.

A Signed Newspaper Article
Hentoff, Nat. "Lawyers for Animals." <u>The Washington Post</u> 28 Apr. 1990: A23.

An Unsigned Newspaper Article
"Lab Animal Protection Broadened." <u>The Washington Post</u> 9 Jan. 1992: A6.

An Editorial
"Making a Great Zoo Even Better." Editorial. Los Angeles Times 21 Sep. 1991:B5.

A Review of a Book, Film, or Performance
Visscher, M.B. Rev. of Animal Rights and Human Morality, by B. E. Rollin. New
England Journal of Medicine 306 (1982): 1303–4.

Models for Other Sources

Government Documents

Government publications sometimes present problems in bibliographic citation.
The following guidelines are to be followed: First, cite the government and the
agency issuing the document. Second, provide the underlined title of document.
If it is a congressional document, include the number and session of the Congress, which house, and the type of document with its number, if it has one. The
following abbreviations are frequently used:

Comm.	Committee
Cong.	Congress
Cong. Rec.	Congressional Record
Doc.	Document
GPO	Government Printing Office
HR	House of Representatives
Res.	Resolution
S	Senate
sess.	Session

Most federal publications, regardless of the branch of government, are published by the Government Printing Office (GPO).

United States. Cong. Office of Technology Assessment. Alternatives to Animal
Use in Research, Testings, and Education: Summary. Washington: GPO,
1985.
United States. Cong. Senate. Subcommittee on Constitutional Amendments of the
Committee on the Judiciary. Hearings on the "Equal Rights" Amendment.
91st Cong., 2nd sess. S. Res. 61. Washington: GPO, 1970.

Interviews

Foreman, Dave. "A Discussion with Dave Foreman of Earth First!" Interviewed
by W. Pacelle. Animals' Agenda 7 (Dec. 1987): 6–9, 52–3.
Safire, William. Larry King Live. Interviewed by Larry King. CNN, Atlanta. 21
Feb. 1990.
Winther, Monique. Interviewed by Sue Mattingly. 5 Nov. 1992.

Lectures and Speeches

Regan, Tom. "The Philosophy of Animal Rights: An Introduction." Eastern Kentucky University, 5 Nov. 1991.

Cartoons and Advertisements

Trudeau, Gary. "Doonesbury." Cartoon. Star-Ledger [Newark, NJ] 27 May 1989: 25.

Films and Television Programs
Gorillas in the Mist. Dir. Michael Apted. Warner and Universal, 1988.
Ice Fox. Nova. PBS. WGBH, 1992.

Letter to an Editor
Roy, Suzzanne E. "We Can't Turn Animals into Parts Shops." Letter to the Editor.
   The New York Times 16 July 1992: A18.

⊙➤   **Suggested Writing Assignment 17**   ⊂⊙

Compose a Tentative Works Cited List
Attach the Evaluation Guide

Collect your sources, locate the appropriate MLA models, create an entry for each source, alphabetize the entries, and compose a draft of your tentative list of works cited. Depending on what sources you actually use in your text, you will add or delete entries as you prepare your presentation copy.

A Model Research Paper

Once you understand the logic of the MLA style of parenthetical documentation, you are ready to write your paper, report your research findings, and document sources. To help you document, the *MLA Handbook* urges you to keep the following two guidelines in mind. First, make sure references in your text clearly point to specific sources in the list of works cited. And second, identify the exact location of borrowed information (156). Note, for example, how Mattingly follows both guidelines as she borrows information and documents her source in the model research paper:

> Philip Abelson reports that the principal method of determining potential carcinogens is based on experiments in which animals are forced to ingest huge amounts of a substance over a period of time—usually the length of the animal's life. Foods such as "apples, bananas, carrots, celery, coffee, lettuce, orange juice, peas, potatoes, and tomatoes" were all found to cause cancer in laboratory rodents" (1357). That these foods were found to cause cancer in animals is surprising, for it has long been established that human diets rich in fruits and vegetables reduce the incidence of human cancers.

First, by explicitly referring to Philip Abelson in her text, Mattingly clearly points to a specific entry in the list of works cited. Second, by putting the page number, 1357, in parentheses immediately after reporting her source's information, Mattingly identifies the exact location of the borrowed information.

As important as it is to follow these two guidelines, the *MLA Handbook* indicates that it is equally important not to overdocument a source by repeating information unnecessarily. "If, for example, you include an author's name in the sentence, you need not repeat it in the parenthetical page citation that follows" (157). In other words, don't make your audience read repeat information.

Often, however, your audience may appreciate knowing the title of a source—especially if it is a book—without having to refer to Works Cited. You may, therefore, give both the author's name and the title of the source upon their first mention. In her research paper, for example, Mattingly identifies both in this introduction to her source:

> According to Peter Singer in <u>Animal Liberation</u>, when the tapes were viewed, they were seen to contain . . .

Giving the title often provides important information that helps your reader put the source in a context.

When incorporating information into your text, it's also important that you use an effective rhetorical marker (like the rhetorically accurate verb in the first sentence of a précis)—some signal verb or signal phrase—that faithfully reflects the author's intentions or the source's tone. In the Abelson example, Mattingly chose the signal verb *reports* because she wants to convey a sense of objectivity on Abelson's part. The nature of your source, the intention of the author you're using, and your decision as to how you will use your source—all these factors will determine what signal verbs or signal phrases you will use. Here is a list of some of the signal verbs and phrases commonly used by researchers:

Signal Verbs

acknowledges	considers	interprets	remarks
advises	criticizes	leaves us with	replies
agrees	declares	lists	reports
allows	describes	objects	responds
analyzes	disagrees	observes	reveals
answers	discusses	offers	says
appreciates	embraces	opposes	states
asserts	emphasizes	points to	suggests
assumes	explains	presents	supports
believes	expresses	proposes	tells us
charges	holds	recognizes	thinks
claims	implies	regards	

Signal Clauses and Phrases
> Abelson asserts that . . .
> As Abelson reports,
> According to Abelson,
> In Abelson's opinion,
> From Abelson's viewpoint,
> In Abelson's report,

Variations
> Although Abelson argues that . . . , Cohen contends that . . .

Examples
> But as Peter Singer informs us, . . .
> Abelson calls such carcinogen testing methods "obsolescent
>   relics . . ."
> Further, Bross confidently reports that . . .
> In addition, Edward F. Dolan, Jr. reports that . . .
> Tom Regan points to evidence that confirms . . .
> Mary Midgley supports this view by saying . . .
> Henry Salt suggests that . . .
> Ingrid Newkirk charges that . . .
> In response to Regan's charge, Cohen insists that . . .

Setting off Long Quotations

When you insert a long quotation into your text, your readers may experience difficulty in seeing it because quotation marks (small as they are) often get lost in the forest of letters. Readers, therefore, sometimes have to reread lines to figure out where a long quotation begins and ends. To help readers overcome this difficulty, you should set off any quotation that turns out to be more than four printed lines. The *MLA Handbook* offers this advice:

> If a quotation runs to more than four typed lines, set it off from your text by beginning a new line, indenting ten spaces from the left margin, and typing it double-spaced, without adding quotation marks. A colon generally introduces a quotation displayed in this way. . . . (Gibaldi and Achtert 58)

Such a blocked quotation needs no quotation marks because the very act of blocking indicates that it is a quotation. Moreover, because long quotations often contain much information, you are urged to write a full sentence by way of introduction to help your readers see what you want them to perceive. Notice, for example, how Mattingly assists her readers by previewing for them what, in fact, they will read in the blocked quotation:

According to the PCRM, research on animals is highly unreliable:

> Many animal experiments produce results that are far from relevant to human health. . . . Animals and humans differ in medically important ways, and often animal experiments can produce misleading results. . . . (The Facts)

When the blocked quotation is preceded by a full sentence that ends with a colon, the reader has two opportunities to take in the information. Such courtesies are much appreciated by readers who often need help when reading new material for the first time.

Improve Your Documentation Style with the Three-Step Method

As you write, you will most likely refer to numerous outside sources to support your ideas. You may quote material word for word, you may paraphrase what someone else has written, or you may summarize entire sections or chapters. In each case, unless the information is common knowledge, you will want to document your use of outside sources.

As a writer, of course, you probably know what you want to say, what your writing is supposed to mean, and what you want your writing to convey. When you are writing an early draft, you produce what some people call a writer-based text. That is, from your point of view, the text makes good sense because it is based on your understanding, your knowledge, and your ability to interpret it.

But a writer-based text is not always a reader-based text. That is, a text that makes sense to you may not always make sense to your readers. As a writer you are in a privileged position: you already are something of an expert on the topic. Your reader, however, may not be as well informed as you nor always able to understand what you mean and want to communicate. It's your responsibility, therefore, always to transform your writer-based text into a comprehensible reader-based text. Being able to make this transformation is especially necessary when you are writing a researched essay. To make sure that you perceive the difference between a writer-based text and a reader-based text, examine the following passages carefully:

A Writer-Based Text

> Over two-thirds of all animal species that have existed have now been wiped off the face of the earth (Hoage 1). Although the processes of extinction continue, we have recently been able to save some species that might otherwise be lost forever. Since the Endangered Species Act has been in effect, seventeen species have been moved from the endangered species list to the threatened species list. An eighteenth species, the gray

whale, has been delisted. There are now more whooping cranes alive than at any other time in this century. Federally supported captive breeding programs have rescued the black-footed ferret, the California condor, and the Guam rail from extinction, replenished their population, and restored them to their protected habitats (DiSilvestro 17).

Notice in this six-sentence passage that it is difficult to tell where the author started using information from DiSilvestro. Is sentence three from DiSilvestro? What about sentences four and five? Without some introductory signal as to where the use of DiSilvestro begins, the reader must guess. Moreover, because the writer appears to be using outside information in every sentence, it's not possible for a reader to determine where the writer is within the paragraph. The writer's voice is hidden among all the apparent paraphrasing.

By contrast, a reader-based text is written to avoid such confusion. Note how one can improve upon a writer-based text by transforming it into a reader-based text:

A Reader-Based Text

The loss of species has been severe. According to R. J. Hoage, over two-thirds of all animal species that have existed have now been wiped off the face of the earth (1). Although the processes of extinction continue, we have recently been able to save some species that might otherwise be lost forever. Roger DiSilvestro reports that, since the Endangered Species Act has been in effect, seventeen species have been moved from the endangered species list to the threatened species list. An eighteenth species, the gray whale, has been delisted. There are now more whooping cranes alive than at any other time in this century. Federally supported captive breeding programs have rescued the black-footed ferret, the California condor, and the Guam rail from extinction, replenished their population, and restored them to their protected habitats (17). Such reversals are heartening. They indicate that we can indeed reverse what once looked like an inevitable process of depletion.

In this rewritten version, the reader knows exactly when and where the author is commenting, when the author begins and ends his use of Hoage, and when the author begins and ends using DiSilvestro. The reader is able to discern three distinct sources of information: the writer's, Hoage's, and DiSilvestro's. Thus, a writer-based text has been transformed into a reader-based text.

To improve your style of documentation, try what some researchers call the three-step method, which helps your readers understand what is happening whenever you incorporate outside facts, ideas, or information into your text:

1. Use an *introduction* that gives the author's name and links the upcoming material to an entry on the works cited page. You have two basic ways to make this introduction:

   A. Use a signal phrase set off by a comma or a signal verb with a "that" clause:

   > According to Peter Singer, whenever there is the possibility of an animal's suffering, we must respond morally (8).

   > Peter Singer contends that, whenever there is the possibility of an animal's suffering, we must respond morally (8).

   B. Use a formal sentence as an introduction that ends with a colon:

   > Peter Singer contends that if animals can suffer, then humans must think morally about such suffering: "If a being suffers, there can be no moral justification for refusing to take that suffering into consideration" (8).

2. Give the quotation, paraphrase, summary, or data, and end with the page numbers of the source in parentheses. Close the passage with a period:

   > Peter Singer contends that if animals can suffer, then humans must think morally about such suffering: "If a being suffers, there can be no moral justification for refusing to take that suffering into consideration" (8).

3. Provide your reader with a coming-away comment, some additional sentence that refers to, explains, or clarifies the secondary material. Thus, for example, after providing a quotation, paraphrase, or summary from Singer, you might provide the following editorial comment so that the entire three-step procedure looks like this:

   > Peter Singer contends that if animals can suffer, then humans must think morally about such suffering: "If a being suffers there can be no moral justification for refusing to take that suffering into consideration" (8). This attitude permeates all of Singer's thinking about the relationship people have with animals.

Such coming-away comments, used when you "come away" from outside sources, serve two important functions. First, they give you an important opportunity to reestablish your own authoritative voice by inserting it into the text. This reestablishment of your voice tells your reader that you are in command of the textual presentation. Indeed, to develop an even stronger voice within your own text, try to conclude all paragraphs with your thinking and your words. Try not to be satisfied with ending a paragraph with someone else's thinking. Instead, write a concluding sentence that summarizes the whole paragraph and brings it to a genuine sense of closure.

Second, with coming-away comments, you help your reader negotiate your text by clarifying where sources are being used. You do not allow your outside sources to run themselves together in a confused manner. Instead, you indicate when you are finished using one source and when you are beginning to use another. By commenting editorially on outside material, you establish yourself as the one who is in charge. And you make it easier for your readers to understand your writing.

Content Notes

Near the beginning of this chapter, it was remarked that "at one time, it was common practice to include footnotes containing information about sources of information or ideas. . . . Today, however, the extensive use of . . . footnotes . . . is not as popular as it once was." While that statement is true, it is not absolutely true. MLA style does allow for the use of so-called content notes with parenthetical documentation. As Gibaldi and Achtert define them, "content notes [offer] the reader comment, explanation, or information that the text cannot accommodate" (176). Content notes thus provide opportunities for short digressions, such as credits to people who helped you in a writing project, an explanation about a research problem, interesting tidbits, and matters of importance that are not germane to your discussion.

For example, in the model research paper, Mattingly uses two content notes. In the first note, she thanks the members of her research team for helping her locate information. In the second note, Mattingly provides more information about Michael A. Fox, the researcher who dramatically changed his mind about the usefulness of animal experimentation. Mattingly chose to provide this information in a content note because she thought that giving the details of Fox's radical change would interrupt the logical flow of her text too much. But because Fox's reversal on the issue of animal experimentation is an important story to tell, she decided to narrate some of it in a content note. Thus, those readers who want more information about Fox can find it in note number 2.

The *MLA Handbook* provides these directions for setting up a content note:

> In providing this sort of supplementary information, place a superscript arabic numeral at the appropriate place in the text . . . and [place] the note after a matching numeral at the end of the text (an endnote). (176–77)

Unless you are told to do otherwise, make all your content notes endnotes. "As their name implies," Gibaldi and Achtert remind us, "endnotes appear after the text, starting on a new page numbered in sequence with the preceding page."

Abbreviations for MLA Documentation

The following list includes some of the abbreviations and reference words commonly used with MLA-style documentation.

ed.	edited by, editor, edition
et al.	*et alii, et aliae* (meaning "and others")
n.d.	no date of publication given
n. pag.	no pagination given
n.p.	no place of publication given, no publisher given
qtd.	quoted by
rpt.	reprinted by, reprint
U	University
UP	University Press
vol., vols.	volume, volumes

It is often not necessary to give a publisher's full commercial name when listing it in Works Cited. When the publisher's name includes the name of one person (for example, Harry N. Abrams, Inc.), cite the surname alone (Abrams). When the publisher's name includes the names of more than one person (Harcourt Brace Jovanovich), cite only the first of these names (Harcourt). Acceptable shortened forms of publisher's names include the following:

Abrams	Harry A. Abrams, Inc.
Allyn	Allyn and Bacon, Inc.
Appleton	Appleton-Century-Crofts
Basic	Basic Books
Bowker	R. R. Bowker Co.
Cambridge UP	Cambridge University Press
Columbia UP	Columbia University Press
Dodd	Dodd, Mead, and Co.
Doubleday	Doubleday and Co., Inc.
Farrar	Farrar, Straus, and Giroux, Inc.
Feminist	The Feminist Press at the City University of New York
Free	The Free Press
Greenhaven	Greenhaven Press
Harcourt	Harcourt Brace Jovanovich, Inc.
Harper	Harper and Row Publishers, Inc.
Harvard UP	Harvard University Press
Holt	Holt, Rinehart and Winston, Inc.
Houghton	Houghton Mifflin Co.
Johns Hopkins UP	The Johns Hopkins University Press
Knopf	Alfred A. Knopf, Inc.
Lippincott	J. B. Lippincott Co.

Macmillan	Macmillan Publishing Co., Inc.
MIT P	The MIT Press
MLA	The Modern Language Association of America
Norton	W. W. Norton and Co., Inc.
Oxford UP	Oxford University Press, Inc.
Princeton UP	Princeton University Press
Rand	Rand McNally and Co.
Random	Random House, Inc.
St. Martin's	St. Martin's Press, Inc.
Scribner's	Charles Scribner's Sons
Simon	Simon and Schuster, Inc.
UMI	University Microfilms International
U of Chicago P	University of Chicago Press
Viking	The Viking Press, Inc.
Yale UP	Yale University Press

4

Expanding Your Research

A library may be defined as an extensive storehouse of information that is classified for quick retrieval. Because a college or university library can provide you with up-to-date information on almost any subject, you need to learn how useful your library can be as a resource center. Most academic libraries provide brochures and booklets designed to help you locate materials. Often these booklets contain floor plans and descriptions of collections that may interest you. Using the brochure, take the time to walk through the library and pay attention to what is available. Ask the librarians for assistance in becoming acquainted with your library. If you are fortunate enough to have a librarian or an instructor introduce you to the library, pay special attention to those library services that may prove invaluable.

Don't be reluctant to become friends with your librarians. In *How to Use a Research Library*, David Beasley offers this good advice:

> Overcome any hesitancy in approaching librarians; they are subject specialists trained to direct you to the correct sources for using the collections. Research librarians not only hold advanced degrees in library science, but often advanced degrees in another field, making them subject specialists in that field as well. As you become familiar with the library and its staff, you will get to know which librarians have the special skills you need to help you in your particular areas of interest. Be explicit in describing your information needs to the librarians. Because librarians are often hard-pressed for time, you should formulate your questions carefully before you ask them. Your ability to describe your research needs clearly enables librarians to give you the full benefit of their knowledge and training. (16)

As you become acquainted with your library, you will probably discover that the amount of information contained in even a modest-sized library reference section is impressive. The list of reference works that follows is, although by no means exhaustive, typical of those sources contained in most academic libraries.

Where Do You Start?

Start with the excellent, up-to-date bibliographies in your Opposing Viewpoints text. These bibliographies are often your first line of information; they contain references to articles and books that most libraries either have or can get for you. Many, for example, appear in popular weekly magazines such as *U.S. News & World Report* and in daily newspapers like the *New York Times*.

For a fast and focused start, begin with the periodical bibliographies that appear either at the end of each chapter or just before the index at the back of your text. Most of the articles are in periodicals, journals, magazines, or newspapers to which your library subscribes. The retrieval format in which the article is available may vary; it may be located in a bound volume, on microfiche, or on microfilm. If your source is on microfilm, use a microfilm reader. Directions on how to view microfilm on a reader and how to obtain photocopies of pages are usually easy to follow. In the event that your library does not subscribe or does not have the issue you're interested in, see about obtaining a copy of the article through the interlibrary loan service.

For more expansive coverage of your topic, carefully review the bibliography of books (usually printed after the listing of organizations to contact in your text) and mark those books that seem particularly relevant. Then, using your library's main card catalog or on-line catalog, locate the call number, check out the book, read, and take notes on whatever seems appropriate for your search.

Another valuable resource in your Opposing Viewpoints text is the annotated list of organizations to contact. All these organizations have publications for interested readers, and the descriptions of their materials have been provided by the organizations themselves. Many of the organizations are well funded and will send quantities of brochures and other information. Some, however, are less well funded and will appreciate reducing mailing costs by sending one set of materials to a designated class member who can share information with others.

You will, in all likelihood, want to obtain more information than that provided by your Opposing Viewpoints text. What you do next will depend on the subject you are researching and how much material is published on it. However, there are some general guidelines that you can follow. First, think about what type of research information you'd like to find. Unless you are doing research that requires you to actually look at past records, books, and statistics (for example, political cartoons of the 1890s), start with the most recently published research and follow that research where it leads you, going back only as far as your study requires. Limiting yourself to research done in the last several years will keep your paper current and accurate. By examining what's been done recently, you will more than likely find yourself being introduced to the past. While reading these up-to-date sources, check to see if they include a list of references. You may find additional sources to examine.

When starting research, it is often a good idea to get an overview of your topic. For example, if your research requires that you examine the history of animal experimentation, you will need to acquaint yourself with several good, broad encyclopedia articles, perhaps even a book on the topic. Don't, however, rely on one source. If you must depend on a single book, article, or several issues of one journal for your information, you may not be able to fulfill your instructor's expectations for doing research. Writing from a single source usually limits you to writing merely a summary. By contrast, writing a fully researched essay requires that you use several—perhaps many—sources so that you must interpret and evaluate facts, opinions, and ideas. If you discover that you are becoming too dependent on one source, ask your instructor how you can turn your research efforts toward more productive ends.

Some research projects may immediately require that you examine a narrow field of study. If, for example, you were to focus your research on the debate about the use of animal experimentation within the cosmetic industry, you might well begin with material devoted exclusively to a discussion of that topic. Writing on a topic that is small in scope allows you to go to work quickly. If you're not sure where or how to begin, talk with your instructor or someone who knows the field well. After all, a good deal of research involves talking initially with those who know where to suggest you go for information.

General Encyclopedias

The number of general and specialized encyclopedias available is astonishing. Indeed, as Kenneth F. Kister reports in *Best Encyclopedias: A Guide to General and Specialized Encyclopedias*, encyclopedias exist for nearly every topic, including film, television, pets and domestic animals, photography, computer science, pop and rock music, medicine, law, business, history, military affairs, economics, political issues, and literature. Among the numerous general encyclopedias, three are especially important:

- *New Encyclopedia Britannica* (1991). This thirty-two-volume set—the *Britannica,* as most people call it—is arranged in three parts: the twelve-volume *Micropaedia* (Ready Reference) contains 61,000 brief articles for quick reference; the *Macropaedia* ("large knowledge"), with 681 lengthier articles, treats selected subjects in depth; the *Propaedia* (Outline of Knowledge) outlines all the material included in both the *Micropaedia* and the *Macropaedia.* A two-volume index accompanies the set.
- *Collier's Encyclopedia* (1990). The articles within this twenty-four-volume set are written with the need of student researchers in mind. Each article is about a thousand words in length. Almost all (98 percent) of the articles are signed. The writing style is typically clear and to the point. As Kister notes, "the encyclopedia's bibliographies, most of which are found at the beginning of volume 24, add a valuable dimension to the set" (47).
- *Encyclopedia Americana* (1990). Written for adults and college students, this thirty-volume encyclopedia aims to be "a bridge between the worlds of the specialist and the general reader" (Preface). Approximately 75 percent of its 52,000 articles are signed. While international in scope, the *Americana* provides more generous treatment of U.S. and Canadian subject areas—geography, biography, history, and institutions. Its style is clear, accurate, and unbiased. It contains an especially effective index.

In addition to providing excellent articles, these general encyclopedias often contain important bibliographies that will list other sources of information about your topic.

Specialized Encyclopedias
Many specialized encyclopedias and other resources on many topics are commonly available. When searching for information, be aware that other sources, such as specialized dictionaries, fact books, handbooks, almanacs, and atlases, also often contain articles and information traditionally associated with encyclopedia entries. The following are appropriate resources for topics (often related to each other) in the Opposing Viewpoints series:

African-American Issues
  Encyclopedia of Black America, 1981.
  The Negro Almanac: A Reference Work on the African American, 1989.

Aging and Elderly Issues
  The Encyclopedia of Aging, 1987.
  The Encyclopedia of Aging and the Elderly, 1992.

Fact Book on Aging, 1990.
Statistical Handbook on Aging Americans, 1986.

Censorship and Civil Liberties Issues
Banned Books, 387 B.C. to 1978 A.D., 1978.
The Encyclopedia of Censorship, 1990.
World Press Encyclopedia, 1982.

Children and Teenage Issues
The Child Care Encyclopedia, 1984.
Encyclopedia of Adolescence, 1991.
Encyclopedia and Dictionary of Medicine, Nursing, and Allied Health, 1987.
Handbook of Child Psychology, 1983.

Criminal Justice Issues
The Encyclopedia of American Crime, 1982.
The Encyclopedia of Crime and Justice, 1983.
The Encyclopedia of World Crime, 1989.

Drug and Chemical Dependency Issues
The Encyclopedia of Alcoholism, 1991.
The Encyclopedia of Drug Abuse, 1992.
The Encyclopedia of Psychoactive Drugs, 1986.

Economic and Trade Issues
Encyclopedia of American Economic History: Studies of the Principal Movements and Ideas, 1980.
Encyclopedia of Banking and Finance, 1990.
Encyclopedia of Economics, 1982.
Encyclopedia of Investments, 1991.
International Encyclopedia of Statistics, 1978.

Educational Issues
American Educators' Encyclopedia, 1991.
The Encyclopedia of Education, 1971.
Encyclopedia of Educational Research, 1982.
Encyclopedia of Special Education, 1987.
Standard Education Almanac, annual.
World Education Encyclopedia, 1988.

Environmental Issues
Encyclopedia of Environmental Science and Engineering, 1983.
The Encyclopedia of Environmental Studies, 1991.
McGraw-Hill Encyclopedia of Environmental Sciences, 1980.

Ethical and Moral Issues

   A Companion to Ethics, ed. Peter Singer. Blackwell Companions to Philosophy.
      Cambridge, MA: Basil Blackwell, 1991.
   The Encyclopedia of Philosophy, 1973.
   Magel, Charles R. *Keyguide to Information Sources in Animal Rights,* 1989.
   World Philosophy: Essay-Reviews of 225 Major Works, 1982.
   World Spirituality: An Encyclopedic History of the Religious Quest, 1985–.

Family and Gender Issues

   Encyclopedia of Adolescence, 1991.
   Encyclopedia of Homosexuality, 1990.
   Encyclopedia of Sexual Behavior, 1973.
   Statistical Handbook on Women in America, 1991.
   What's the Difference? How Men and Women Compare, 1985.
   Women's Studies Encyclopedia, 1989.

Health Issues

   Encyclopedia of Bioethics, 1982.
   Encyclopedia of Death, 1989.
   The Encyclopedia of Health.

International Issues

Africa

   The African Political Dictionary, 1984.
   The Cambridge Encyclopedia of Africa, 1981.
   Encyclopedia of the Third World, 1992.

Central America

   The Cambridge Encyclopedia of Latin America and the Caribbean, 1992.

China

   The Cambridge Encyclopedia of China, 1991.
   Encyclopedia of Asian History, 1988.
   Worldmark Encyclopedia of the Nations, 1988.

Israel

   Encyclopedia of the First World, 1990.
   Encyclopedia of Jewish History, 1986.
   Encyclopedia of Judaica, 1972.
   The New Standard Jewish Encyclopedia, 1992.
   Political Dictionary of the State of Israel, 1987.

Japan

   Concise Dictionary of Modern Japanese History, 1984.
   Encyclopedia of Asian History, 1988.
   Encyclopedia of Japan, 1990.
   Kodansha Encyclopedia of Japan, 1983.

The Middle East
  The Atlas of the Arab World: Geopolitics and Society, 1991.
  The Cambridge Encyclopedia of the Middle East and North Africa, 1988.
  The Middle East: A Political Dictionary, 1992.
  The Middle East Political Dictionary, 1984.

The Soviet Union
  The Cambridge Encyclopedia of Russia and the Soviet Union, 1982.
  The Dictionary of Marxist Thought, 1983.
  The Soviet and East European Political Dictionary, 1984.

The Third World
  Encyclopedia of the Third World, 1992.
  The Marshall Cavendish Illustrated Encyclopedia of the World and Its People, 1986.
  Worldmark Encyclopedia of the Nations, 1988.

Political and Foreign Policy Issues
  The American Political Dictionary, 1992.
  A Companion to Contemporary Political Philosophy, ed. Robert E. Goodin and Philip Pettit. Blackwell Companions to Philosophy. Cambridge, MA: Basil Blackwell, forthcoming.
  Dictionary of American Diplomatic History, 1989.
  Dictionary of American Immigration History, 1990.
  Dictionary of Concepts on American Politics, 1980.
  Dictionary of Political Thought, 1984.
  Encyclopedia of the American Constitution, 1990.
  Encyclopedia of American Foreign Policy: Studies of Principal Movements and Ideas, 1978.
  Encyclopedia of American Political History: Studies of the Principal Movements and Ideas, 1984.
  Encyclopedia of Political Science, 1989.
  The Ethnic Almanac, 1981.
  Harvard Encyclopedia of American Ethnic Groups, 1980.
  The International Relations Dictionary, 1988.
  The Latin-American Political Dictionary, 1980.
  The Presidential-Congressional Political Dictionary, 1984.

Religious Issues
  Abingdon Dictionary of Living Religions, 1981.
  The Encyclopedia of American Religions, 1989.
  Encyclopedia of the American Religious Experience, 1988.
  The Encyclopedia of Religion, 1986.
  New Catholic Encyclopedia, 1967.
  World Christian Encyclopedia: A Comparative Study of Churches and Religions in the Modern World, 1982.

Science Issues
Asimov's New Guide to Science, 1984.
Concise Encyclopedia of the Sciences, 1982.
The Dictionary of Dreams: 10,000 Dreams Interpreted, 1985.
Dictionary of the History of Science, 1981.
Encyclopedia of the Biological Sciences, 1981.
Encyclopedia of Computer Science and Technology, 1975–.
Encyclopedia of Occultism & Parapsychology, 1991.
Growing Up with Science: The Illustrated Encyclopedia of Invention, 1984.
Grzimek's Encyclopedia of Evolution, 1976.
International Reference Work in Fifteen Volumes Including an Index, 1992.
Larousse Encyclopedia of Astrology, 1980.
McGraw-Hill Concise Encyclopedia of Science and Technology, 1989.
McGraw-Hill Encyclopedia of Science and Technology: An International Reference Work in Fifteen Volumes Including an Index, 1992.
The New Book of Popular Science, 1984.
Van Nostrand's Scientific Encyclopedia, 1983.

Value Issues
Compendium of American Public Opinion, 1988.
Editorials on File.
Encyclopedia of Adolescence, 1991.
Encyclopedia of Aging, 1990.
Encyclopedia of Alcoholism, 1991.
Encyclopedia of the American Left, 1990.
Encyclopedia of Bioethics.
Encyclopedia of Child Abuse, 1989.
Encyclopedia of Death, 1989.
Encyclopedia of Drug Abuse, 1992.
Encyclopedia of Gambling, 1990.
Encyclopedia of Homosexuality, 1990.
Encyclopedia of Marriage, Divorce, and the Family, 1989.
Encyclopedia of Psychology, 1984.
Encyclopedia of Suicide, 1988.
Gallup Poll Monthly.
Handbook of American Popular Culture, 1989.
Lamm, Kathryn. *10,000 Ideas for Term Papers, Projects and Reports.* New York: Arco, 1987.
Pro & Con, 1983.

War and Peace Issues
Civil War Dictionary: A Concise Encyclopedia, 1959.
Encyclopedia of the American Revolution, 1974.
The Encyclopedia of Military History: From 3500 B.C. to the Present, 1986.
The Illustrated Encyclopedia of Twentieth Century Weapons and Warfare, 1979.
The International Relations Dictionary, 1988.
Nuclear Weapons Databook, 1984.
Spy/Counterspy: An Encyclopedia of Espionage, 1982.

This list of encyclopedias does not nearly include everything available; hundreds of specialized encyclopedias have been published, and many libraries maintain extensive holdings in such research tools. The *Master Index to Subject Encyclopedias* (1989) provides "a keyword and broad subject index to nearly 40,000 topics in 430 of the best sources of background information and topic overview. . . . Sources include English-language subject encyclopedias, dictionaries, handbooks, comprehensive textbooks and other 'standard sources' in all subject areas" (Preface). If you cannot readily find sufficient background information on your topic, consult the *Master Index* and ask your reference librarian what's available.

Special Bibliographic Resources
Computer Searches
Many libraries provide computer data bases that are user friendly and exceptionally helpful to researchers. For example, InfoTrac, one of the more popular data bases, provides two major data bases. The first is the *Expanded Academic Index* that indexes 960 scholarly and general-interest publications and one newspaper—*The New York Times*. The second, *The National Newspaper Index*, is a one-stop source that searches references from *The New York Times*, *The Christian Science Monitor*, *The Wall Street Journal*, *The Los Angeles Times*, and *The Washington Post*.

CQ Researcher
CQ Researcher, formerly *Editorial Research Reports*, is a research service that reports and analyzes current issues of national significance. For convenient reference, weekly reports are stored chronologically in a three-ring binder, which holds a year's worth of reports. In addition, reports are reissued every six months in a hardcover volume, providing a cumulative, permanent edition of the reports. To assist researchers, each report contains a brief summary on the front cover, thorough footnotes, and a supplementary reading list of books, articles, and studies pertaining to that week's topic. On the back cover of each report is a chronological list of report titles from previous months, providing a quick snapshot of recent coverage. A subject index, going back five years, is contained in the bound volumes published every six months.

Educational Resources Information Center (ERIC)
ERIC is a national education information system developed and maintained by the National Institute of Education. This comprehensive system is involved with the collection and dissemination of educational resources. Abstracts and indexing are provided in *Resources in Education*, and the complete text of most titles is available. This system may be searched on CD-ROM.

Congressional Hearings

Greenwood and CIS are two microfiche collections that provide coverage for almost all congressional committee hearings held since the early 1930s. Abstracts and indexes give subject analysis and the names of individuals who appeared before the committee. Hearings contain current information not easily found elsewhere.

American Statistics Index

This is a comprehensive indexing and abstracting service that provides access to the multitude of statistical tables published in federal agency publications. It is the most detailed and up-to-date source for statistical data.

Biographical Dictionaries

All of the books in the Opposing Viewpoints series make frequent mention of important people, living and dead, who have made significant contributions to the topic you're investigating. Thus, for example, when doing research on the philosophical ideas about the rights of animals, one is invariably introduced to two scholars: Peter Singer and Tom Regan. To familiarize yourself with an author, consult an appropriate biographical dictionary, perhaps one of the following:

Biography Index. 1946–. Published quarterly; provides biographical information found in current books and over twenty-six hundred periodicals; its on-line and CD-ROM data bases begin with July 1984.

Current Biography. 1940–. Published monthly (with annual bound volumes); contains articles on people in current events and often includes photographs and short bibliographies.

Contemporary Authors. 1967–. Published annually, providing short biographies of those who have published works during the year.

Dictionary of American Biography. 1943–. With supplements; contains biographies of more than fifteen thousand deceased Americans from all phases of public life since colonial days; entries include bibliographies.

International Who's Who. 1935–. Published annually, providing information about persons of international status.

Notable American Women: 1607–1950. 3 vols. 1972, with supplement, *Notable American Women: The Modern Period*, 1980.

Who's Who. 1849–. Published annually, providing information about well-known British people.

Who's Who in America. 1899–. Published biannually, providing information about famous Americans.

Indexes

Indexes are guides to articles in magazines, professional journals, and newspapers. Some indexes provide abstracts or short summaries of articles, books, and research papers.

General Indexes
  General Science Index
  Humanities Index
  InfoTrac (automated)
  Monthly Catalog of United States Government Publications
  National Newspaper Index (automated)
  The New York Times Index
  Reader's Guide to Periodical Literature
  Social Sciences Index

Specific Indexes
  Biological and Agricultural Index
  Business Periodicals Index
  Education Index
  Educational Resources Information Center (ERIC) (automated)
  General Business File (automated)
  Pais International in Print

Yearbooks
  Encyclopedia Americana Annual
  Encyclopedia Britannica Book of the Year

Atlases
Atlases not only contain important maps, they frequently provide excellent narratives on geography, culture, politics, and so forth. For example, *The Atlas of the Arab World: Geopolitics and Society* (1983) supplies information on Arabic ethnic groups and religions, population studies, social practices, agriculture, the role of the state, and issues of regional unity.

Fact Books
  Fact Book on Aging
  Statistical Abstract of the United States
  Statistical Handbook on Aging Americans
  Statistical Handbook on Women in America

Current Opinion
  Editorials on File
  The Gallup Poll Monthly
  Opinion?

Vertical Files
Many libraries maintain current vertical files of clippings from newspapers, magazines, and pamphlets organized under subject headings.

Special Collections

One excellent source of information may be your library's collection of videotapes. Such resources are often housed in departmental units with designations such as Instructional Media and Media Resources.

IN SUMMARY

Your library contains most of the information you need to do research. With encyclopedias, bibliographic resources, indexes, yearbooks, fact books, and special collections, it provides indispensable material and services that few researchers can do without. You should, therefore, make every effort to know your library well. If, however, your library does not have the material you need, ask whether it can borrow them from another library. If your library provides interlibrary loan services, consult the *National Union Catalog* to find out which libraries have the books you want or, if you need periodicals, the *Union List of Serials* and *New Serial Titles*. Most libraries have mutual agreements that make the exchange of research materials on a regional, state, or national level quick and easy.

The more you know about the library and the materials and services it provides, the more successful you will be in gathering information and ideas for your research paper.

5

Taking Notes

Once you have located your sources and have them in hand, your next step is to read them and, taking notes, store whatever information you gather for possible use when composing your paper.

There is no one way to take notes. For reading whole essays and digesting their essential content, writing rhetorical précis, making dialectical notes, or doing charted readings works very well. But when the time comes to collect information that you may use in your paper, what works for you may not work for someone else. As a consequence, everyone has to find his or her own method. In addition to dialectical note taking, the composing of rhetorical précis, and creating charted readings, you have many other options for note taking. Decide for yourself which of the following methods will work for you and use that system to collect information.

Use Note Cards

This standard method still works well for those who know how to use it to their advantage. One good piece of advice is to use cards that are at least 4″ x 6″. You may even prefer to use 5″ x 8″ cards because larger cards generally allow you to write down all the information on one card.

Students using note cards generally divide them into two kinds: 1) those for a working bibliography and 2) those with content information. Working bibliography cards are used primarily to create a later entry in your list of works cited; content cards are used to record pieces of information and are keyed to a working bibliography card.

Working Bibliography Cards

Whenever you use a source of any kind, write down all of its bibliographical data on a separate card. To create a working bibliography for a book, record the following information:

Author, editor, or both
Title and subtitle, if any
Publisher's name and location
Year of publication (from the copyright page)
Any other important information: translator, edition, and so forth
Page numbers where information is located
Library call number or other location information

Here's an example of a working bibliography card containing information on a book Sue Mattingly used while working on her research paper:

```
Langley, Bill, ed. Animal
Experimentation: The
Consensus Changes. New York:
Chapman and Hall, 1990.

HV 4915 . A65
```

To create a working bibliography card containing information about an article, record the following information:

Author
Article title and subtitle, if any
Periodical name
If appropriate: volume number
Date
Inclusive pages for the article
Available format and location

Mattingly prepared this working bibliography card for an article:

Fox, Jeffery L. "Lab, Break-in
Stirs Animal Welfare Debate."
Science 22 June 1984:1319-20.

When creating a working bibliography card for a book or article (or any other source), always double-check your card for accuracy.

Content Cards

Content cards are written to record ideas, quotations, paraphrases, summaries, data, and other information that you think will be useful in your presentation. It's generally a good idea simply to record only one piece of information on each card. Label each card with a descriptive heading and always write out the author's name or some other identifying marker that will refer you to the more complete working bibliography card.

When it comes time to actually make a content card, you will save lots of time by doing the following:

- Write down enough information so that you can recollect the significant points of your source.
- Try to put down the information in the same way you think you might use it later in your text.
- Be sure to key your content card to your working bibliography card so you can cite your source accurately in your works cited listing if necessary.

On the following content card, Mattingly paraphrased and quoted information from Jeffrey Fox's article:

ALF *breaks into* U Penn *lab*

On *Memorial, Day, 1984, five members of the Animal Liberation Front (ALF) entered the vacant head-injury laboratory at the University of Pennsylvania Medical School and ruined over $20,000 worth of laboratory equipment. The group also "stole video tapes that the laboratory had created while filming some of the experiments" (1319).*
Fox, Jefferey. "Lab Break-in"

If you commit yourself to this system, you will discover that you can easily arrange and rearrange your content cards by their descriptive headings in whatever order seems best when actually writing the text and incorporating sources.

Here's another strategy. Devise a system to key your cards to a specific writing project. Take the writing project suggested in this book as illustration. Knowing that you will write six sections—background, lines of argument, refutation, introduction, conclusion, and Works Cited—you can also "key" information from rhetorical précis, quotations, statistical data, paraphrases, or summaries to a particular section of your paper. Here, for example, are the symbols Mattingly devised to key information to her text:

INTV = interview   Q = quotation
MA = major argument   SUM = summary
PI = paragraph idea   WB = Working Bibliography
PRP = paraphrase   WC = Works Cited

Mattingly, after reading Stephen Kaufman's "Most Animal Experimentation Does Not Benefit Human Health" in *Animal Rights: Opposing Viewpoints*, prepared the content card (facing page) for her background section.

As a researcher, you are free to devise your own system of symbols and notation, and no doubt you can tailor your system to the particular needs of your own writing project.

Draize Test/Unsound

*"The Draize eye irritation test, in which un-
anesthetized rabbits have substances in-
stilled in their eyes, is scientifically unsound.
...When Draize data for 14 household and
cosmetic products were compared to accidental
human eye exposures, they differed by a
factor of 18 to 250" (75).
Kaufman, Stephen. "Most Animal Experimentation
Does Not Benefit Human Health." Rohr 75.*

Use a Research Journal or Notebook

Some students, wishing to keep all their notes closely bound together, prefer to use a research journal or notebook. With this method, you use any sort of binder with pages and write down information much as you would for note cards. Generally, the author and title are recorded at the top page, and everything taken from that source is written below and on subsequent pages.

Photocopy Material

Whether you use cards or a notebook, you will most likely photocopy some material in order to save time copying information by hand. When you do so, *always* remember to mark each copy with the author's name or some identifier that keys the copy to a working bibliography card that provides complete information about its source. If you use something from your photocopy to help you write your own text, you will need this bibliographical information to make an entry in the works cited listing. In some cases, you may want to copy the title page and the copyright page of a book and attach it to your photocopies.

The problem with photocopied pages is that they are often hard to arrange, rearrange, or file because page sizes are often frustratingly large. One way to solve this problem is simply to use five or six file folders (or notebook dividers) and label them: background, lines of argument, refutation, and so on. Keep information for the background section in the background folder, and so forth. Another useful suggestion is to reduce the material on the photocopier so that you have more room in your margins to make brief notes as to how you intend to use the material.

Interviewing with a Tape Recorder

Because interviews are such a rich source of information, it is a good idea to use a tape recorder when conducting one. After the interview, transcribe whatever material you judge to be useful into some form of notes.

As you become more experienced and expert at note taking, you will soon learn to develop a system that works well within your own distinctive writing process.

Quoting, Paraphrasing, Summarizing

It isn't always easy to know exactly what to take notes on. For the beginner in the initial stages of research, nearly everything looks quotable, interesting, and useful. But that's not necessarily the case. What looks worth quoting may turn out to be quite commonly known among certain readers. For this reason, it's wise to get acquainted with your topic generally by skimming through several sources before settling into serious note taking. By reading in and around your subject, you will soon get a sense of the territory, a better idea of the relative value of the information you can find.

Once, however, you are oriented to your topic and ready for note taking, you have, as Gibaldi and Achtert in the *MLA Handbook* indicate, "generally speaking, three methods of note-taking: summary, paraphrase, and quotation":

> Summarize if you want to record only the general idea of large amounts of material. If you require detailed notes on specific sentences and passages, but not the exact wording, you may wish to paraphrase—that is, to restate the material in your own words. But when you believe that some sentence or passage in its original wording might make an effective addition to your paper, transcribe that material exactly as it appears word for word, comma for comma. Whenever you quote from a work, be sure to use quotation marks scrupulously in your notes to distinguish between verbatim quotation and summary or paraphrase. Keep an accurate record, [perhaps] in the left-hand margin, of the page numbers of all material you summarize, paraphrase, or quote. (21)

These are exceptionally useful options. By summarizing, you can describe and condense large blocks of information, perhaps an entire book, into a concisely written paragraph, perhaps even several sentences. On a more local scale, you can paraphrase "specific sentences and passages" by converting them into your own words. This tactic allows you to use a source and yet maintain your own authorial voice and control in doing so. At the same time, you can also give your readers a true sense of the original by making your paraphrase about the same length as the original. Both summarizing and paraphrasing are strategies that you will want to employ to relay information quickly and effectively.

Quotations allow you to introduce another speaker into your text. While such a strategy is "often effective in research papers," the *MLA Handbook* reminds us, we should also, it warns, "use them selectively":

> Quote only words, phrases, lines, and passages that are particularly interesting, vivid, unusual, or apt, and keep all quotations as brief as possible. Overquotation can bore your readers and might lead them to conclude that you are neither an original thinker nor a skillful writer. (56)

That's sound advice. If you simply string quotations together, you in effect turn over your own voice and authority to an often noisy collection of utterances. Your writing will be far more authoritative and convincing if you judiciously let others speak on your behalf. Indeed, some instructors suggest that, for research papers, no more than 10 percent of your text should be given over to quotations. Perhaps that figure is too low. But surely you get the point. Do not let quotations bear the burden of your message. Instead, introduce quotations to reinforce what you want to say. To be persuasive, you must stay in charge. Let others help you make your arguments, but be the master of your paper.

A brief note about ellipses and brackets: When you need to alter a quotation to fit the demands of your writing, you can use ellipses (for example. . .) and brackets (that is [ ]) to help you. Ellipses indicate that you, as a writer, have omitted something from somebody else's quotation; brackets indicate that you have inserted something to help the quotation make more sense to the reader. To see how these two editorial markers work, examine Mattingly's paper in Appendix A, where she frequently employs both indicators.

6

Structuring Your Paper

The spectrum of opinions one may hold on any issue is extensive. By now, if you have critically read and made notes on the introduction and several essays in your Opposing Viewpoints text, you may have some idea as to where you stand on a given issue. Perhaps you have what Peter Elbow and Pat Belanoff in *A Community of Writers* describe as a "felt sense" for your point of view:

> Felt sense may seem a vague concept, but we *get* new leverage in our writing if we realize that there is always *something* there "in mind" before we have words for it. In one sense, of course, we don't *know* something until we have it in words. But in another sense we do indeed know quite a lot, and it's a question of learning to tap it better. . . .
>
> "Felt sense" is what Eugene Gendlin has named this internal awareness that we call on. And his point—which we want to emphasize—is that we can learn to call on it better. (126–27)

Even though you may not be absolutely sure about your position, you can often rely on your felt sense to give you an early indication about your developing point of view. If that's the case, go with your so-called gut feelings about an issue. As Elbow and Belanoff note:

> [Maybe] you haven't *got* a thesis yet—haven't got the right words yet—but you do have a genuinely available feeling for what you are trying to get at. If you check any trial set of words against that feeling, you can tell whether or not they are what you were trying to say. (127)

Your next step is to formulate an assertion, a thesis that reflects your conviction or, perhaps, your growing hunch that one viewpoint is more reasonable than others. Such a conviction or suspicion can, of course, be open to revision at some later date with more information and critical thinking. Be that as it may, most researchers find it helpful to begin their research with some proposition or contention that they'd like to defend. If later research contradicts this assertion, then the original viewpoint will necessarily be rejected, qualified, or somehow improved upon. Nevertheless, a thesis—even a tentative thesis—is a necessary beginning for writing a research paper.

A thesis makes a proposition so that something can be considered. A thesis puts forward a statement for development, for consideration or for evaluation. A thesis makes a declaration or an announcement. A thesis sets down a proposition, especially one to be proven and maintained against objections. In short, with a thesis you take a stand.

Obviously, then, a thesis cannot be a question, no matter how interesting a question. A question or a series of questions may lead up to a thesis, but the thesis itself must be a declaration. A thesis is an emphatic, strong assertion. It leaves no doubt as to what is being set forth. A thesis is a full and complete sentence—or perhaps a series of sentences. It is never a fragment. A strong thesis puts forth the central idea of an essay. It leaves no doubt in the reader's mind as to what you will prove as a writer. A thesis is, thus, not merely an introduction to an idea; it is the single most important component in an essay. A good essay must have one; a superior essay has a superior thesis. Thus, in evaluating an essay, one must inevitably make an evaluation of the thesis: Does it set forth a challenging and provocative idea? Does it go beyond the merely obvious? Does it demonstrate that a thoughtful mind is at work?

Because a thesis actually predicts, previews, and demonstrates, in usually one or two sentences, what a whole essay will contain, it must itself contain all the key ideas of an essay. For example, you may want to prove that the LD-50 (lethal dose 50 percent) test, commonly administered to lab animals to measure toxicity levels of commercial substances, is an inadequate testing procedure. It isn't enough to say, "The LD-50 is a poor test," or "Administering the LD-50 is unjustifiable." While either statement may be defensible, neither one shows exactly how you intend to prove that your assertion is true. You must add, therefore, the key supporting ideas by which you intend to develop your central statement. Here, for example, is how you might really tell your reader what your thesis is:

> The LD-50 test, which attempts to ascertain the toxicity of substances such as pesticides and household products, is no longer scientifically justified because we now know that different species react differently to substances and that reactions between individuals of the same species can vary greatly.

With this thesis, your reader knows exactly and precisely what your essay will try to prove.

Writing a Thesis That Is Committed to One Side of an Argument

Admittedly, as James A. Reinking et al., in *Strategies for Successful Writing*, point out, it is possible to write about something without using a thesis:

> Not all papers have explicit thesis statements. Narratives and descriptions, for example, often merely support some point that is unstated but nevertheless clear, and professional writers sometimes imply their thesis rather than state it openly. Nonetheless, a core idea underlies and controls all effective writing. (27)

Research papers, however, usually contain more than narratives and description. They also address controversial issues and frequently express an opinion. Their purpose is to persuade readers that one point of view is better than another. When a research paper takes a stand, both the writer and the reader need and appreciate a well written thesis.

Writers value theses because they help control the development of their papers. Consider, for example, the thesis that student Sue Mattingly wrote for an argumentative paper on animal experimentation:

> The use of animals in biomedical research frequently impedes medical progress, and the importance of such research is greatly exaggerated by those who support it.

This thesis obligates her to fulfill two responsibilities: First, she must establish that animal experimentation often stands in the way of medical progress; second, she must disprove the claim some people make for using animals in research. As a contract, this thesis requires that arguments for and against an issue be made.

While it's difficult to tell anyone exactly how to compose a thesis, it's sometimes helpful to remember that certain elements are common to many theses. Theses for argumentative research papers often contain auxiliary verbs like *should* or *must*, which indicate that a set of arguments will persuade the reader to some proposal or action. By using the word *should* for example, the following two theses unambiguously argue for different positions:

1. We should try to reduce the use of animals in medical research because there are alternatives.
2. We should continue the use of animals in research because we need to pretest drugs before administering them to humans.

These theses, although opposed, are clearly emphatic in their assertions, and no reader can misunderstand their point of view.

As the examples above indicate, theses also often use the word *because* to introduce the reasons that support the controlling idea. Here, for example, is one such thesis:

> Polygraph tests, as they are currently used by private businesses, should be abolished as a condition of employment because they are intrusive, demeaning, and often inaccurate.

The word *because* forces the writer to state precisely what reasons will be adduced to prove that polygraph tests should be abolished.

When writers take a strong position in opposition to some other viewpoint, they frequently use an "although" construction to make the contrast apparent. Someone arguing that school-based health clinics should not dispense condoms might compose a thesis like this one:

> Although certain groups still advocate the free distribution of condoms in the health clinics of public schools, our recent experience indicates that such a policy is wrongheaded, dangerous to public health, and detrimental to sound moral practice.

This "although" construction compels the writer to state both sides of the issue and then prove that one side possesses the better arguments.

Writing a Thesis That Is Not Committed to One Side of an Argument

In recent years, some writers have noted that not all theses have to support argumentative essays, that is, traditional essays in which authors must be highly committed to proving themselves right. Traditional theses, rhetoric specialist Virginia Perdue suggests, encourage the notion that most good ideas are fixed and should be "defended by one person against the competing ideas of another" (138). Perdue challenges this traditional conception of the thesis and asks us to consider other possibilities. Instead of being doctrinaire or committed to a single answer, can we be free—as writers of research papers—to speculate, create hypotheses, explore, and ask questions that perhaps have no clear answers at the moment? After all, Perdue reasons, sometimes it takes a long time to become really convinced of something. To help you see her point, Perdue asks that we think about a situation comparable to writing:

> Most people, upon walking into a room where a conversation has been occurring, listen first, of course, but when they feel comfortable enough to speak, what are the likeliest forms of those first attempts? Questions, requests for clarification, and tentative offerings, particularly if that newcomer is female, minority, working class, or young—groups which include the majority of students. (140)

Perdue is right. You, in fact, may not want to be committed to a traditional thesis that sets out to prove that one argument is better than another. As Perdue admits, there's nothing inherently wrong with that— "the [traditional] thesis is a useful tool of argument," she says (141), but it may not be the right instrument for your purposes and ideas. For example, most students, if they are working on the abortion topic, tend to believe either that they need to defend abortion and be prochoice or that they need to be antiabortion and defend the right to life. It would seem as though the issue requires that sort of choice: either you are for abortion or you are against it. But suppose you don't know if you are definitely for or against abortion. Some polls have shown, for example, that while most Americans think a woman has a right to have an abortion, they also believe that most abortions are morally wrong. Here, for example, is how Rachel Richardson Smith, a mother and theology student in North Carolina, describes her viewpoint:

> I cannot bring myself to say I am in favor of abortion. I don't want anyone to have one. I want people to use contraceptives and for contraceptives to be foolproof. I want people to be responsible for their actions; mature in their decisions. I want children to be loved, wanted, well cared for.
>
> I cannot bring myself to say I am against choice. I want women who are young, poor, single or all three to be able to direct the course of their lives. I want women who have had all the children they want or can afford or their bodies can withstand to be able to decide their future. I want women who are in bad marriages or destructive relationships to avoid being trapped by pregnancy. . . . I find myself in the awkward position of being both anti-abortion and pro-choice. ("Abortion, Right and Wrong," *Newsweek* 25 March 1985: 16)

Smith has discovered that she affirms what have traditionally been thought to be incompatible ideas and values. After examining her dilemma, she concludes by reflecting: "I wonder how we can begin to change the context in which we think about abortion." In response to this question, one student writer wondered if both prochoice and prolife people could sit down and try something new. In attempting to answer that question, she proposed this thesis:

> Although those who argue for and against abortion seem to be absolutely opposed to each other, nevertheless it may be possible for both sides to find ways to join hands with their adversaries—to push for better prenatal care, adoption reform, and help for drug-addicted pregnant women.

Rather than arguing for a single position and defending that position against all others, this thesis works for a reconciliation of opposing viewpoints. It asks those who disagree about abortion to explore new options. Because both groups profess respect for the integrity of human beings, the thesis wants to explore whether or not these traditional foes can combine their energies to help pregnant women and improve adoption policies. It doesn't seek to prove itself right; rather, it is searching for new possibilities. Thus, although the thesis is not argumentative in the traditional sense, it is nonetheless a good one: it's provocative, interesting, and well worth exploring.

If you think your thesis might somehow be less than traditionally argumentative, read "Present Your Viewpoint," later in this chapter, paying special attention to comments on the Rogerian style of argumentation. You may be able to write and support a thesis that attempts to maintain a dialogue, one that is nonconfrontational in tone. That doesn't mean you will support your thesis with unsound thinking. You will, of course, use your best thinking as you explore ideas that attempt to reconcile opposing points of view, to negotiate new ways of thinking, and to ask "What if?" Like the traditional research paper, your paper will have a clear and emphatic thesis. That it may be different lies in the possibility that, as Perdue suggests, it may "articulate the most thoughtful questions, not necessarily the most certain answers" (141).

The Quality of a Thesis

The strength of an effective expository essay, no matter what its length, depends first on the quality of its thesis. A thoughtful thesis makes it possible to write a superior essay. To check the quality of your thesis, see if it fulfills the following requirements:

- It expresses your position in an emphatic, full, declarative sentence.
- It formally announces the plan of your essay.
- It indicates the purpose of your writing and the degree to which you are committed to presenting information and making arguments.

Your thesis, when well crafted, provides you with a plan for writing even as it predicts and previews for the readers what they can anticipate to be the major idea and design of your essay.

Although it's not easy to tell when it's exactly the right time to write a thesis statement, Gibaldi and Achtert in the *MLA Handbook* suggest that "when you have concluded your research for the paper, it is time to shape the information you have at hand into a unified, coherent whole" (26). Some instructors may disagree by arguing that you don't really have to *conclude* your research in order to compose a thesis. Indeed, if you have a pretty good idea as to how you are going to argue and if you know that further research will firm up your argument, it may be a good idea to draft your thesis while you are in the middle of doing research. Many writers simply trust their intuition and allow later research to confirm their initial feelings. Actually, Gibaldi and Achtert suggest that your thesis may change and evolve into something else as you discover new ideas through writing: "Since the experience of writing may alter your original plans, do not hesitate to refine the thesis statement as you write the paper" (26). That advice can be made even stronger: don't hesitate to *refine or redefine* your thesis.

Let your research be your guide. If, in the middle of exploring opposing viewpoints, you discover that you are on the right track, go straight ahead, stick with your thesis, and support it. If, however, you find that your research is taking you to an opposite set of conclusions, don't hesitate to change your mind, rewrite your thesis, and support your new and better understanding as best you can. If you do rework your thesis significantly, remember always to keep your instructor informed about any changes you are contemplating. Indeed, inasmuch as most instructors require students to submit a thesis statement for approval several weeks before a paper is due, you should talk over with your instructor any major changes you intend to make.

It's also important to recognize that, for some writers, a thesis does not come easily. If that's the case with you, talk with your instructor about your difficulty, describe the research you have done, and indicate what you want to say; with such information, your instructor can probably help you frame an appropriate thesis statement.

☞ **Suggested Writing Assignment 18** ☜

**Write a Thesis That You Will Support
in Your Research Paper**
Attach the Evaluation Guide

Compose a thesis suitable for your research topic. Be sure your thesis meets all the criteria for a strong thesis. Remember: your thesis will obligate you to develop every key idea it contains.

The Structure of an Argumentative Research Paper

Aristotle once pointed out that "a whole is that which has a beginning, a middle, and an end." Aristotle's insight means that all readers want to pass through three experiences to achieve a sense of wholeness while reading. First, they want an introduction to help them know when they are beginning something that will have a middle and an end. Second, readers want to know exactly when they are in the middle of something.

To satisfy this need, we provide transition signals like *first, second,* and *third* in the middle of essays. Finally, readers want to know when they are leaving a particular experience. For this reason, we write conclusions. In short, readers enjoy essays that are well defined.

One of the best structures you can use to deliver and support an argument is that of a five-part presentation known in classical times as an *oratio,* an "oration" or "speech." Because it has been used so often and proven to be so helpful, it continues to be a valuable scaffold upon which you can build an argumentative essay. Indeed, you probably have read or heard someone using it without being consciously aware of it. Many editors, television commentators, politicians, lawyers, and advocates of causes use it daily as their basic format for presenting an argument.

Part 1 is the introduction that draws your readers into the essay. You want to "hook" them so that they want to continue reading. As you come to the end of your introductory section, you provide your readers with your thesis: the major contention and the ideas that support it.

Part 2, the background section, is noncontroversial. It gives a basic orientation to the topic, providing readers with a general overall view. This section should furnish your readers with a context, a framework within which they can place the argument. Establish some common ground upon which you and your readers can stand. To do this work, you have a number of options. You can supply a historical sketch that helps your readers understand the present issues. You can provide statistical data that give your readers an understanding of the scope and importance of the topic. You can define a key term so that your readers have good mental images of what you're writing about. Remember: in this part of your essay, you want to orient your readers to the larger picture.

Part 3, the lines-of-argument section, defends your thesis. In this section, you present the important reasons that support your thesis proposal. This is probably the most important section of your essay. Each supporting reason should be carefully developed.

Part 4, the refutation, presents the opposing points of view. To the best of your ability, fairly state the arguments that others will make against your thesis. Then, show why and how such opposing arguments are, in fact, weak, inadequate, or wrong. In the refutation, you refuse to let an opposing point of view have any overwhelming weight or power.

Because the refutation makes you responsible for articulating both sides of an argument, Robert Connors and Cheryl Glenn, two well known writing instructors, suggest that students using the five-part structure be able to list at least two arguments that their opposition would be likely to use before they begin to write; otherwise, they say, their refutation sections could be too general or indistinguishable from their previous lines-of-argument sections (217). By writing two rhetorical précis that summarize articles written by those who oppose your point of view, you should be able to meet the minimal requirements for writing an effective refutation. You will, of course, then have to disprove and discredit your opponents' point of view. In parts 3 and 4, you take the offense and then hold your own against objections.

Part 5, the conclusion, rounds off your essay and brings it to completion. You should briefly remind readers of what they have experienced in reading your essay. You may want to tell a final brief story. You may want to encourage your readers to do something, to take some action.

To see how an argumentative essay can be developed, note how Mattingly designed her essay by letting her thesis control its structure:

Does Animal Research Really Benefit Human Health?

  I. Introduction: The use of animals in biomedical research frequently impedes medical progress, and the importance of such research is greatly exaggerated by those who support it.
 II. Background section
     A. Historical beginning
     B. Current use of animals in experimentation
     C. The number of animals used
     D. Those who support experimentation
     E. Those who oppose experimentation
     F. Brief history of protests
     G. Public opinion
     H. What new awareness would do
III. Lines-of-argument section: Use of animals frequently impedes medical progress.
     A. Problems of transferability
     B. Problems with reliability
     C. Funds could be better spent on alternatives
 IV. Refutation: Those who support such research exaggerate its importance.
     A. The whole story is often not told
     B. Examples
        1. Link between pancreas and diabetes
        2. Statistical evidence
        3. Discovery of antibiotics
     C. Physicians' Committee for Responsible Medicine: clinical studies have produced the most significant advances

V. Conclusion
   A. Clinical studies—most valuable tool
   B. Why the continued use of animals?
      1. Inertia of medical community
      2. Desensitized scientists
   C. Change is taking place.

(The outline Sue Mattingly prepared for her research paper)

As this outline demonstrates, in addition to framing her research paper with an introduction and conclusion, Mattingly provides an informative background, supports her thesis with arguments, and discredits the opposing point of view in her refutation.

○➢   **Suggested Writing Assignment 19**   ✐○

Work Out the Structure for Your Research Paper
Attach the Evaluation Guide

Draft a reasonably detailed (and admittedly tentative) outline that will govern the structure of your essay. Give your outline a tentative title. Place the thesis statement underneath the title. Underneath the thesis statement, provide an outline of your paper. Remember that the descending parts of an outline are normally labeled in the following order:

I.
  A.
    1.
      a.
        (1)
          (a)
          (b)
        (2)
      b.
    2.
  B.
II.
Logic requires that there be a *II* to complement a *I*, a *B* to complement an *A*, and so forth.

Present Your Viewpoint

Part 3, the lines of argument, is the most critical section of your essay. In this section, after providing helpful background information, you support, in order of importance, the main contentions of your essay. If in the thesis, for example, you listed reasons to support your major assertion, you develop each supporting reason in the lines-of-argument section. You present a series of arguments to persuade your readers that your thesis is worthy of acceptance.

When presenting your viewpoint, choose a style of argumentation that best suits your thesis. Many writing teachers, as Nevin K. Laib observes in *Rhetoric and Style*, "make a distinction between monologic and dialogic argumentation—often called Aristotelian and Rogerian after the classical rhetorician Aristotle and the modern psychologist Carl Rogers" (292). The Aristotelian argumentative style has the following characteristics:

- It is combative, adversarial, and confrontational.
- It piles up evidence, closes off communication, and sees the opposition as misguided.
- It emphasizes winning and generally recognizes only one truth.
- It tends to polarize or politicize the debate, to push people into opposite camps.
- It sees truth and justice in black-white terms.

"The Aristotelian style," says Laib, "is not so much aimed at persuading the person who disagrees with you as at overwhelming that person" (292–93). To determine if your writing will be characterized by an Aristotelian style of writing, examine the following sets of questions. If you answer yes to one or more of the following questions, you will likely want to use an Aristotelian style of argumentation.

- Do I need to be highly assertive?
- Must I control the floor or the agenda?
- Do I need to cut off further discussion?
- Must I build an airtight case to defend my position?
- Do I need to refute, ridicule, or criticize the opposition?
- Does the issue require that I maintain certain principles that cannot be given up?
- Can I appeal to my audience's emotions and come away with integrity?
- Must I come across as precisely logical for the sake of my point of view?

The Aristotelian style of argumentation emphasizes three ways to convince readers. First, it uses logic and appeals to your readers' sense of reason. The style examines an issue thoughtfully and puts on an impressive display of critical thinking. Second, it demonstrates that, as a writer, you are a person who observes high ethical standards. You demonstrate, for example, that you have thoroughly researched the topic. You have been rigorous in your investigation of the facts. Third, the style manipulates your readers' feelings. Depending on the situation, it uses tactics that either calm or stir up your audience's emotions. For example, if strong emotions have clouded an issue, you place your readers in a more objective frame of mind. If, however, they seem not to care, you raise their awareness so that they respond with some passion for your position. By using logical analysis, your own ethical point of view, and readers' emotions, you attempt to persuade them to your point of view.

By contrast, the Rogerian style is less calculating, less aggressive, more gentle, and open to dialogue. It assumes, Laib suggests, that *"both* sides in a dispute can have good reasons for believing as they do" (293). A Rogerian presentation of argumentation possesses these features:

- It tries to persuade rather than argue.
- It attempts to maintain a dialogue and is, therefore, communal and nonconfrontational in tone.
- It seeks to listen and to explain because it respects opposing points of view.
- It emphasizes understanding and allows for pluralistic truths.

In the Rogerian style, the author makes an effort to understand that someone can have a different opinion; in fact, the author might even try to paraphrase a counterargument to be sure of understanding it well. Such a style is sometimes satisfied by partial solutions and compromises. Surprisingly, however, it is not necessarily less assertive. Although it may fail when perceived as weak or manipulative, ultimately "it may," Laib emphasizes, "be more effective in achieving lasting and productive results" than would the more obviously confrontational Aristotelian style.

As you develop your ideas and reasons to support and to oppose arguments, you will need to determine which style best suits you, the issues, and your audience. On the one hand, the monologic Aristotelian style conveys the positive qualities of independence of thought, command of reasoning, resolute attitude, and self-assurance; on the other hand, to some audiences it may also suggest a lack of consideration, an autocratic mind, a dogmatic attitude, and a self-serving author. But the dialogic approach also has its own built-in benefits and liabilities. Some may perceive a Rogerian presentation as considerate, engaging, and cooperative; others may see it as unctuous, servile, and uncritical. To see if the Rogerian style best suits your needs, ask yourself the following questions:

- Can I show respect for the opposing point of view?
- Can I accept differences of opinion and perspective?
- Do I need to please my audience?
- Must I qualify my beliefs?
- Can I afford to be seen as flexible and compromising?

If you answer yes to one or more of these questions, you may want to consider using a Rogerian presentational style. You emphasize, for example, that you genuinely understand and appreciate your opponent's point of view. You may even admit that it makes sense from a certain point of view. You use nonthreatening language to avoid setting up polarities. You offer suggestions to move the discussion forward. Your own ethical character is not the main focus of attention. You indicate that you and your reader may both want to change. You encourage everyone to revise his or her image of the world. The tone of your presentation suggests that you and your readers can, and should, be changed through the process of mutual inquiry.

Once you have formed some overall policies about how you will present yourself and your arguments, you will be more nearly ready to write your paper. It should, of course, be based on solid research and reliable information.

Suggested Writing Assignment 20

Write Part 3 of Research Paper (Lines of Argument)
Attach the Evaluation Guide

Support your thesis by presenting reasons to convince your readers that your point of view or proposal is credible. In doing so, you may do one or more of the following:

- Narrate a personal experience
- Speculate about or predict an outcome
- Defend a position or conclusion
- Solve a problem
- Analyze or evaluate a situation, person, place, or thing
- Explain a process or concept
- Propose a model or plan

Use the MLA style of documentation when incorporating outside material in your text. It is not necessary to write an introduction or conclusion to your lines-of-argument section. As the third part of a larger writing project, the lines-of-argument section will be placed immediately after the background section and before the refutation.

Refute Opposing Arguments

Most issues worth debating are highly complex and demand thoughtful consideration of opposing viewpoints before one can understand, think through, and be persuasive about one particular viewpoint. Understandably then, your readers may want to know both sides of an issue before they make up their minds as to whose arguments are best. It is for this reason that you must honestly inform your readers of opposing points of view and help them understand why you think your thesis and supporting arguments are better. Richard Paul, in *Critical Thinking: What Every Person Needs to Survive in a Rapidly Changing World*, describes your task as a writer:

> To think critically about issues [you] must be able to consider the strengths and weaknesses of opposing points of view; to imaginatively put [yourself] in the place of others in order to genuinely understand them; to overcome [your] egocentric tendency to identify truth with [your] immediate perceptions or longstanding thought or belief. (404)

Even if you disagree with your opponents' viewpoints you must strive to be fair-minded. Take no easy or cheap shots by misrepresenting those who disagree with you. Represent fairly the ideas of those who disagree with you, noting both the advantages and disadvantages of opposing views.

Once you have fairly articulated the opposing point of view, you may rebut it. If you are arguing in an Aristotelian fashion, aggressively discredit, disprove, and refute your opponents' arguments. Take the opposing arguments apart and show how or why they are wrong. Attack your opponents' logic and show that it is fuzzy, wrongheaded, inadequate, poorly reasoned out, and perhaps ethically bankrupt. Using your best logic and what others have said in support of your thesis, demonstrate that your side of the issue is more reasonable, sound, and clearheaded. In short, *refute* the counterarguments.

If, however, you have chosen to use the more moderate, Rogerian style of argument, then you may choose a more diplomatic approach to win your audience's approval. This strategy may even prove to be more helpful in the long run, especially when you are arguing about matters of policy and procedure. It may even be possible to find ways to bring out the best in both viewpoints and work toward a compromise. Such exploration—based on compromise, mediation, and truce finding—are not part of a refutation, in the strictest sense of the word. If you use such discourse in your argumentative essay, it might be better called the *reconciliation*.

☞   ## Suggested Writing Assignment 21   ☜

Write the Refutation
Attach the Evaluation Guide

Show your reader that, even though you understand your opponents' points of view, your arguments and point of view are more credible and acceptable. Or show your reader how a reevaluation of arguments may move the discussion beyond traditional polarities.

7

Making Your Presentation Effective

CREATE A TITLE

The title of your paper is the first part of your introduction. Because the title contains the first words that all readers see, as editor Richard Leahy points out, it "often works in concert with the opening paragraph," and inasmuch as "the purpose of the opening paragraph is to get the reader interested and show where the essay is going, the title usually does the same" (516). To make your title work more closely with your introduction—and by extension, the whole essay—Leahy suggests the following exercise as a way to discover what might become the best title for your paper:

1. Copy out of your draft a sentence that could serve as a title.
2. Write a sentence that's *not* in the draft to use as a title.
3. Write a title that is a question beginning with *What, Who, When* or *Where.*
4. Write a title that is a question beginning with *How* or *Why.*
5. Write a title that is a question beginning with *Is/Are, Do/Does,* or *Will.*
6. Pick out of the essay some concrete image—something the reader can hear, see, taste, smell, or feel—to use as a title.
7. Pick another concrete image out of the essay. Look for an image that is a bit unusual or surprising.
8. Write a title that begins with an -ing verb (like "Creating a Good Title").
9. Write a title beginning with *On* (like "On the Title of Essays").
10. Write a title that is a lie about the essay. (You probably won't want to use this one, but it might stimulate your thinking.)
11. Write a one-word title—the most obvious one possible.
12. Write a less obvious one-word title.
13. Write a two-word title.
14. Write a three-word title.

81

15. Write a four-word title.
16. Write a five-word title.
17. Think of a familiar saying, or a title of a book, or movie, that might fit your essay.
18. Take the title you just wrote and twist it by changing a word or creating a pun on it.
19. Do the same with another saying or title of a book, song, or movie.
20. Find two titles you've written so far that you might use together in a double title. Join them together with a colon. (517)

While doing this exercise won't "*guarantee* good titles," Leahy notes, it can lead to promising results and will generally improve the quality of one's title (518). Because your title should make a strong first impression, be easily understood, and interesting, if not provocative, you should give it your best consideration.

In the presentation copy of your paper, center the title on the first page above your first paragraph. Capitalize those words in your title that would be capitalized in any other title. Articles (*a, an, the*), prepositions, conjunctions, and the *to* of an infinitive are not capitalized unless they are the first or last words in a title or subtitle. Neither underline your own title nor put quotation marks around it.

Write the Introduction

Even though an introduction comes at the beginning of a piece of writing, it is not always the first thing to be written. In fact, many writers hold off writing an introduction until they have a better idea as to how the whole paper is going to shape up. Then, once they see the project in its entirety, they set about writing an introduction. You, too, may have delayed writing your introduction. But, if your project's thesis and supporting material have already been drafted, you may want to start writing an introduction as soon as possible. Since you know what your readers will be reading, as a writer you can more easily compose an introduction that will invite them to read it. After all, it's always easier to introduce something or someone you already know.

Etymologically, *introduction* means "a leading into." By getting your reader's attention, your introduction invites the reader to "come on in and read." Like the promotional preview of a film designed to get an audience into the theater, your introduction should make your reader want to keep on reading. If it helps, you can even think of your introduction as the first strands of a web (which is exactly what the classical Romans called it—an *exordium*, that is, "beginning a web" that will ensnare your reader.

Ideally, an introduction tries to accomplish three tasks: First, it gets the reader's attention; second, it announces what your writing will do; and third, it establishes your credibility as a writer and spokesperson for a cause or argument.

There are, of course, many ways to capture your readers' attention, and experience has proven that it's generally best to create an introduction that will be attractive, compelling, perhaps even irresistible. Here are some possibilities:

- Show that your topic is interesting, curious, fascinating, or capable of raising provocative questions. Perhaps you can tell an anecdote, inform your reader about something he or she knows little about, or use an arresting quotation to gain your reader's attention. If writing about illiteracy, you might, for example, share this statistical information provided by Jonathan Kozol in *Illiterate America* (1985):

  > Twenty-five million American adults cannot read the poison warnings on a can of pesticide, a letter from their child's teacher, or the front page of a daily paper. An additional 35 million read only on a level which is less than equal to the full survival needs of our society. Together, these 60 million people represent more than one-third of the entire adult population. (4)

These surprising statistics, when given in an introduction, will prepare most readers to accept a thesis urging that full-scale efforts are needed to eliminate illiteracy.

- Show that your topic has been misunderstood, neglected, or misrepresented. Perhaps you can demonstrate that your topic will change the way people perceive or understand something.

  > Buddhism is not a pessimistic religion; extending a hand of welcome to all forms of life, it cultivates the recognition of goodness in all sentient beings and urges humans to live with compassion and wisdom.

Presumably, the thesis to follow will attempt to persuade those who know little about Buddhism to adjust their perceptions about an ancient religion commonly misperceived in Western cultures.

- Show that your topic gives rise to important questions, significant ethical concerns, or serious consequences. Perhaps you can suggest that new information now throws a changing perspective on your topic:

  > Recent research into animal communication suggests that it may be inappropriate to judge nonhuman animal language by our limited experience of speech and writing. The more we understand animal conversations, the less we will set ourselves up as the privileged aristocrats of evolutionary development.

By setting the stage for what appears to be a thesis that reduces mankind's privileged positions, this introduction immediately suggests that its readers may soon experience new ways to think about human life.

As Winifred Bryan Horner makes clear, "Gaining the attention of the reader is especially important in writing, since readers will quickly turn the page or move on to something else if [you] have not caught their interest in the first or second paragraph" (235). Once, however, you have gotten your reader's attention, your next responsibility is to tell the reader what your paper is all about. That, of course, is the function of your thesis. Many rhetoricians suggest that the best place to state your thesis is at the *end* of your introduction. If your introduction is one paragraph, then try closing that introductory paragraph with your thesis. If your introduction requires more than one paragraph, put your thesis at the end of the last introductory paragraph.

Here's why. Your beginning paragraphs should contain your main idea (the thesis) and present it to best advantage. The clearest and most emphatic place for your thesis sentence is at the end—not at the beginning—of the opening paragraphs. Sheridan Baker explains:

> If you put it first, you will have to repeat some version of it as you bring your beginning paragraph(s) to a close. If you put it in the middle, the reader will very likely take something else as your main point, probably whatever the last sentence contains. The inevitable psychology of interest, as you move your reader through your first paragraph(s) and into your essay, urges you to put your thesis last—in the last sentence of your beginning paragraph.
>
> Think of your beginning paragraph, then, not as much as a frame to be filled, but as a funnel. Start wide and end narrow. (44)

By funneling down to your thesis, bring your reader first into your essay and *then* preview what he or she will read. Because readers like to be treated courteously and with respect, they will appreciate an introduction that first welcomes them into the essay and then explains what will happen.

When your introduction wins your readers' attention and effectively informs them exactly of what your writing will do, you are well on your way to success. You have completed two-thirds of your introductory work.

To make your introduction effective, you still need to convince your readers that they can trust you; that is, you need to establish your credibility, your integrity. You have to establish ways to stand behind every word you write so that your readers learn to trust you. Establishing your credibility may be the most difficult task to accomplish. Obviously, you can't simply say, "Trust me!" and expect your audience unconditionally to accept every word you write. It's much harder than that. Indeed, sentence by sentence, you must establish a trusting relationship with your readers. To do that, as Horner reminds us, you need to show your audience that you are intelligent, virtuous, and goodwilled. First, demonstrate your intelligence by a careful presentation of your expert knowledge. You sound reasonable. You don't exaggerate. You allow for doubts and uncertainties. And you acknowledge other viewpoints. Second, recommend yourself as a virtuous person inasmuch as you like to identify yourself with other people who have integrity. You fit yourself, by your choice of words and arguments, within a larger community of concerned people. The sources that you quote should have reputations that command respect. Finally, you exhibit goodwill by being mindful of your audience. You are courteous, if at all possible, with those who disagree with you. Indeed, you reach out to find common ground wherever possible. You respect your readers even when they disagree with you. In short, you present yourself as a person of good character (54-56).

Because it is important to make a strong first impression, begin to entice your reader, preview your arguments, and prove yourself credible with the first sentence in the introduction. Thus, while the introduction is not nearly as long (it may be simply a paragraph, perhaps two) as the other sections of your paper, in its own way writing the introduction is as challenging as writing other parts of your paper.

You, of course, can meet the challenge of an effective introduction because as a researcher you already possess all the necessary knowledge to present yourself as an expert on your topic. Moreover, having worked hard to fairly understand the context and all major points of view, you respect both those who agree and disagree with you. The familiarity you possess with your subject, the strength you have acquired by associating with thoughtful people, and the thoughtfulness with which you have written so far will prove a solid foundation upon which you can write your introduction. Prepare to write the lead in and weave the web that catches your audience; then write the opening section of your paper.

Suggested Writing Assignment 22

Create a Title for Your Writing Project
and Write the Introduction
Attach the Evaluation Guide

Work through Leahy's twenty suggestions and create a title for your writing project. In a short paragraph, indicate why you think your choice of a title is a good one. Write the introduction. Make a strong opening impression. Get your readers' attention and place your thesis at the end of your introduction.

Write the Conclusion

In many ways you have, in fact, been writing conclusions throughout your paper. Indeed, to create a reader-based text, you have probably framed most paragraphs so that the interior supporting material is introduced with *topic sentences* and rounded off with some sort of appropriate *closure*. You have concluded each of your paragraphs with appropriate closures because you know that your readers need help in moving from one idea to the next as they negotiate your text. You realize that your readers need and appreciate brief summaries, sometimes placed at the end of paragraphs, sometimes at the end of sections, by which you remind them of what has been said and developed.

Because your readers need to know when they are coming to the end of your essay and its argument, you also need to provide closure for your entire essay. When discussing the end of an essay, the classical Roman rhetoricians called this section a *peroratio*. Edward P. J. Corbett in *Classical Rhetoric for the Modern Student* explains the word:

> The common Latin term for this part was *peroratio*, a word which in the prefix *per-* suggested "a finishing off" of one's plea. What the Latins meant by "finishing off" is suggested by the two heads under which [they discussed the] peroration—*enumeratio* (an enumeration or summing-up) and *affectus* (producing the appropriate emotion in the audience). (307)

If we fail to sum up ideas for our readers or leave them dangling and not knowing what to do or feel, then we are merely stopping the essay and not really ending it. In the conclusion, then, we recapitulate in yet another interesting manner what we have already said. A recapitulation is a recapping, a summary, or concise review. In short, we remind our readers of the essay's thesis.

If at all possible, however, avoid writing a routine ending that simply restates the thesis. Although the temptation to write such a conventional ending can be great, especially when you're nearly finished with your entire project, a copycat ending can make an otherwise fine essay disappointing. To go beyond simply rephrasing your introduction, you have several options:

- In addition to restating your thesis, you can leave your readers with something to ponder, perhaps a question that arises naturally out of your representation.
- After restating your thesis, you can make a recommendation that something be done in response to your point of view. You can advise your readers about what they can do next if they are convinced that your thesis is worthy of support.

Suggested Writing Assignment 23

Write the Conclusion
Attach the Evaluation Guide

Provide a satisfying conclusion to your writing project. In summing up the essay, perhaps give your readers more to think about and encourage them to respond to the implications and significance of your thesis.

Final Editing

If you are like most students, you will give your instructor the presentation copy of your essay near the end of the semester. That product, when you deliver it, will be the conclusion of a long process often marked with frustration, anxiety, trepidation, fear, and worry. In response to comments by your instructor (and perhaps by peers), you have already revised portions of your paper. By taking sections of your paper through multiple drafts, you have restructured, tightened sentences, and rephrased much of your first- and second-draft writing. Before you are ready to turn in a presentation copy, however, you must reread and edit your work. As good as your work may be, it can still be improved.

Many books—such as Joseph M. Williams's *Style: Ten Lessons in Clarity and Grace*, and Claire Kehrwald Cook's *Line by Line: How to Edit Your Own Writing*—provide ample advice on revising and editing. While such books are helpful, they often contain so much advice that students find themselves overwhelmed. To help solve that problem, Carolyn Mulford, managing editor of *Writing Concepts: The Newsletter on Writing and Editing*, suggests six basic editing strategies that will help all writers.

1. *Read your verbs.* Run your finger down the page and say the verbs as you come to them. "They should summarize what's on the page. If you can't tell what you've written from the verbs, go back and strengthen them."

Use precise, active verbs whenever possible. Don't use a form of the verb *to be* if you can avoid it. If you must use the passive voice, know why. Check all verbs modified with an *-ly* word. Wherever possible, replace such combinations with a single verb.

2. *Look for periods.* Draw a slash after every sentence. Then analyze the lengths of sentences for a pattern by asking these questions: Do all the sentences run the same length? Do they divide into short, medium, and long or long, longer, and longest?

The results, Mulford suggests, indicate whether you have varied not only the length of your sentences but also the structure and rhythm. If you see a problem, check the way you've begun each sentence—phrase, independent clause, dependent clause. Even looking at the first word of each sentence may help. If each (or almost all) begins with *The, A(n)* or one proper name, rewrite.

It won't hurt to check the paragraphs to make sure you have varied the length and the opening word.

3. *Circle prepositional phrases.* A series of such phrases, especially three or more in a row, will often confuse readers. By circling prepositional phrases, you alert yourself to the problem. Here, for example, is a sentence troubled by too many prepositional phrases:

> The financial statements and related data presented elsewhere in this report have been prepared in accordance with the generally accepted accounting principles, which require the measurement of financial position and operating results in terms of historical dollars without regard to changes in the relative purchasing power of money over time.

Such a sentence, as Mulford describes it, "looks like it suffers from chicken pox." It's hard to read. With most of the prepositional phrases eliminated, its message is easier to comprehend:

> Following generally accepted accounting principles, this report states the company's financial position, operating results, and related data in historical dollars, disregarding changes in purchasing power.

Eliminating chains of prepositional phrases has shortened the original by 50 percent. Such editing will also shorten and clarify your own writing.

4. *Underline transitions.* Writers who clearly see connections between ideas often assume that their readers also perceive them. "The transitions," as Mulford explains, "remain in the writer's head, and leave the readers scratching theirs. The absence of underlining warns a writer to put those links on the paper."

While it's possible for skilled writers to move from one idea to another by using subtle transitional devices (such as echoing a key word from a previous paragraph), students generally improve their texts by including the following transitional phrases:

- In narration and process analysis, words that express time relationships: *after, again, during, every time, first, next, second, the next day, then, while*
- In description, words that express spatial relationships: *behind, in back of, inside, on the left side, on top, over, under*

- In comparison, words that express relationships of likeness: *also, comparable, either . . . or likewise, neither . . . nor, similarly*
- In contrast, words that express relationships of dissimilarity: *but, however, in comparison, in contrast, more, on the one hand, on the other hand, rather, unlike, less*
- In cause-effect analysis, words that express relationships: *as a result, because, consequently, hence, therefore, thus*
- In examples, words that signal that an example or illustration is to follow: *as, for example, for instance, like, such as, thus, to illustrate, with respect to*

5. *Measure the readability of your text.* If after checking verbs, sentence lengths, prepositional phrases, and transitions, you still feel uncertain about your manuscript, you may clarify the problem by assessing its readability. The term *readability* usually refers to reading age for which a piece of writing is appropriate. While some computer programs like *Grammatik IV* and *Writer's Helper* provide a way to measure writing levels, you can do it yourself with Robert Gunning's Fog Index, which he developed for a wire service to use in testing the grade level (the density of the fog) of its material. As Mulford describes it, the formula involves four steps:

> In a passage of 100 words (that makes the arithmetic easy), count the number of sentences and find the average number of words per sentence; count the hard words (those three syllables or longer that aren't proper nouns or lengthened by prefixes, suffixes or the combination of simple words); add the two figures; multiply by .4. In theory, but not always in fact, the answer gives you the grade level of the writing.

To see how the formula works, observe how the following one-hundred-word passage from a typical paragraph of the model research paper is analyzed:

> Recently, however, animal rights activists have questioned the argument that medical progress depends on the use of animals in biomedical research. Does animal research really benefit human health to the degree that some scientists claim? The answer is often "No," and the logic supporting this response appeals not only to our compassion for other creatures, but also to our intellect as well. The use of animals in biomedical research frequently impedes medical progress, and the importance of such research is greatly exaggerated by those who support it.

> According to E. Westacott, animal experimentation began as early as 100 A.D.

This passage contains 5 sentences; the average number of words per sentence is 20; there are 12 hard words. The total for the average number of words per sentence plus hard words is 32. Multiplying 32 by .4 gives us the number 12.8—or about 13—the grade level of this text.

Once you have determined the readability of your text, you weigh the results against the grade level of the audience for whom you are writing. Inasmuch as 14 is the grade level for college sophomores, it would appear as though the readability of this text is appropriate to its audience.

6. Finally, before you finish, Mulford suggests that you give your paper "the breath test."

> To do this, read the paper aloud. If you run out of breath before you get to punctuation, start cutting or dividing up your sentence. If you hyperventilate from breathing at every stop or pause sign, your rhythm is jarring. You may want to write in a stacatto rhythm for short stretches to create a certain reaction in the reader, but long passages will discomfort the reader. Revise to improve the flow. . . . If you get lost in a sentence, or in a paragraph, and don't know where to place the emphasis, you will confuse and lose your audience. If you find yourself droning on with little inflection or change of pace, you need to vary sentence structure. If you don't relish the sound of some of your words as you say them, you probably chose dull words that will bore your reader. (2)

Mulford's advice is good. Using your ears when you write improves the quality of your writing.

It may not be necessary to go through all of these steps for all of your writing. It is a good idea, however, to consider using them when you feel unsure about your writing in general or about your research paper. As suggestions for editing, the six steps will serve you well.

Prepare the Presentation Copy

When you have almost finished, you will know what Lunsford and Connors mean when they say, "One of the satisfying parts of the writing process is the preparation of your final manuscript" (705). If you have done your work with a computer, you will find that printing the presentation copy is a pleasant and rewarding final task.

To make sure that your presentation copy satisfies the MLA's format for a research paper, observe the following requirements:

- Double-space all lines consistently throughout the entire paper.
- Type or print on one side of the paper. If your instructor accepts handwritten work, make sure it is neat, written with a dark-blue or black-ink pen, legible, and written on only one side of the paper.
- Use 8½" x 11" white paper.

- Except for page numbers, leave one-inch margins at the top and bottom and on both sides of the text. (Computer printers usually maintain these margins automatically.)
- Indent the first word of a paragraph five spaces from the left margin.
- Indent blocked quotations ten spaces from the left margin.
- You do not need to create a title page. Beginning one inch from the top of the first page and flush with the margin, type in your name, your instructor's name, the course number, and the date on separate lines, double-spacing between the lines. Double-space again and center the title. Double-space also between the lines of the title, and double-space between the title and the first line of the text.
- Do not underline or put your title in quotation marks; do not type it in all capital letters. Follow the rules for usual capitalization of titles.
- Number all pages consecutively in the upper-right corner, one-half inch from the top. Type your last name before the page number. If possible, use the so-called header and page-number functions of your word processor. Do not put parentheses or hyphens around the page numbers. Do not use the word *page* before the page number.
- For tables and illustrations, see directions on page 27.
- Proofread your presentation copy carefully. If your instructor allows corrections, write them neatly above the lines involved using carets (^) to indicate where they go.
- Do not use a plastic binder unless your instructor requires one. Secure the pages with a paper clip. Do not fold down the corners; do not fasten the pages with staples or pins.
- If required, place the writing to be evaluated in an appropriate portfolio binder or folder. Place all other supporting materials (photocopies of articles, earlier drafts, and so forth) in the folder as directed.
- If required to do so, attach evaluation guide or any other cover sheet provided by your instructor.

⊟⇨   **Suggested Writing Assignment 24**   ⇦⊟

Prepare the Presentation Copy
Attach the Evaluation Guide

After carefully editing and proofreading the entire paper, prepare the presentation copy. Follow the format requirement of the MLA style for a research paper.

Write a Letter of Reflection

A letter of reflection is a final piece of writing in which you evaluate and comment on your own work. In this letter you *reflect* on what has happened to you as a writer while working on your research paper. One of the best ways to make this reflection is to go through your work, assignment by assignment, to see what evidence you find for making observations about yourself as a writer. You might write to your instructor in answer to one or more of the following questions:

- What did you learn (or not learn)?
- How have you improved (or not improved)?
- What discoveries did you make about yourself as a writer?
- What insights have you gained about writing?
- How have you changed as a writer?
- How and why do you see writing differently now?
- How confident are you about your writing?
- How might you improve as a writer?
- What sort of writing is or is not important to you?
- What did engaging in research do for you?
- How has this writing project differed from others?
- What have you learned about doing research?
- Why do you think you should pass this course (or earn an A or B, or whatever)?

You can keep the tone of this letter conversational if you wish. Try, however, to turn this task into a valuable piece of informative writing by which you persuade your instructor that you have carefully reflected upon your work.

✎   ## Suggested Writing Assignment 25   ✎

Compose a Letter of Reflection

Before writing this letter, think over and evaluate the contents of your research paper. Consider the skills you have developed and analyze those areas in your writing process that you feel still need attention. Indicate what writing assignments reflect your best work, review how they were written, and what, if anything, you would change about them. Explain why you believe your portfolio contains writing that deserves a passing grade. Place your letter of reflection on top of the presentation copy of your research paper.

Suggested Writing Assignment 26

Submit Your Search Paper Portfolio

If required, make sure you attach assignment sheets, drafts, revisions, evaluation guides, presentation copy, photocopies of sources, and other relevant material. Remove nonessential materials such as class notes and other handouts. Double-check that all papers pertaining to one assignment have been grouped together.

APPENDIX A

Model Research Paper

The following model research paper demonstrates the MLA style of documentation. Written by freshman student Sue Mattingly, it is based on the work she did for a writing class that used one of the books in the Opposing Viewpoints series—in this case, *Animal Rights*. As a member of a class research team that investigated opposing viewpoints about using animals in medical research, Mattingly employed a five-part structure to present and defend a thesis, cited a wide variety of sources, and demonstrated how they may be effectively incorporated into a research paper.

94

Sue Mattingly

Professor Harnack

ENG 102: 34098

December 13, 1992

Does Animal Research Really Benefit

Human Health?

"Vivisection. . . . It's shock-

ing . . . and blinding, and maiming,

and burning" shrieks <u>Vivisection</u>, a

pamphlet published by the American

Anti-Vivisection Society (AAVS). On

the cover is a picture of a laboratory

rat, implanted with an electrode that

protrudes from the top of its head.

Most of us react with repulsion and

pity. However, animal researchers

quickly remind us of the logic behind

such cruelty--without such animal

experimentation medical progress will

stop and many humans will die. Scien-

tists urge us to consider the sick

children and adults who depend on

animal research to relieve their suf-

Double-space text consistently

Ellipsis indicates omission of original material

Type dash as two unspaced hyphens

2

fering or save their lives. The suffering of laboratory animals can easily
be justified, they contend, by the alle-
viation of human suffering that results
from animal research.

Recently, however, animal rights
activists have questioned the argument
that medical progress depends on the
use of animals in biomedical research.
Does animal research really benefit
human health to the degree that some
scientists claim? The answer is often
"No," and the logic supporting this
response appeals not only to our compassion for other creatures, but also
to our intellect as well. The use of
animals in biomedical research frequently impedes medical progress, and
the importance of such research is
greatly exaggerated by those who support it.[1]

According to E. Westacott, animal
experimentation began as early as 100
A.D. The first physicians, believed to
be the Greeks and Hindus, regularly

Thesis concludes introductory section

Raised numeral refers reader to Notes page(s)

Background section begins here

practiced surgical techniques by per-
forming operations on dead animals
(10). Since then, the practice of
animal experimentation has grown considerably and now includes the use of
conscious or anesthetized animals in
research--often referred to as <u>vivi-
section</u>.

Animals are now used for virtually
every kind of experiment imaginable,
many for testing the toxicities of
poisons, household cleaners, and
caustic substances. According to
People for the Ethical Treatment of
Animals (PETA), the Lethal Dose 50
(LD-50) test is one experiment that
employs animals as models for human
beings. A substance is "forced by
tube into the animals' stomachs, or
through holes cut into their throats"
until 50 percent of them die--"usually
in about two to four weeks." Numer-
ical toxicity indexes are then calcu-
lated before the products are sold
(<u>LD-50 Tests</u>). The LD-50 is but one

Number pages
in upper right
hand corner

The author
integrates
quotation with
her own
sentence
structures

4

of the many toxicity tests using animals that is still applied today.

Other experiments are performed to
test the effectiveness of new drugs and
medical procedures. Animals are
infected with various viruses, they are
implanted with cancers, artificial
hearts and kidneys, or they are surgi-
cally altered so that the diseases or
medical procedures can be studied in
more detail. As Peter Singer reports
in Animal Liberation, Robert J. White
of the Cleveland Metropolitan General
Hospital is "the perfect example of the
scientist who thinks of a laboratory
animal as a tool for research."
Studying the human brain, White experiments on the decapitated heads of mon-
keys that are "alive in fluid" (75).
While White's studies may sound
bizarre, they are but one example of
biomedical research employing animals
as subjects.

The industry and technology of
animal research has grown significantly

5

in the United States during the last
forty years, and conservative figures
estimate the number of animals used
annually in research to be about 3 million (Singer 53), whereas the American
Medical Association (AMA) has noted
much higher figures--15 million in 1986.
Further, the AMA estimates that only 2
percent of laboratory animals used are
cats, dogs, and nonhuman primates; the
remainder are rodents, farm animals,
and birds (61). Whatever the actual
figures are, it is certain that the
number of animals used is very large.

As could be expected, research of
this scope, involving this many animals, has evoked an enormous controversy. Among those who support animal
research are several organizations.
For example, the AMA has always supported the use of animals in research,
as do the National Institutes of Health
(NIH) and the California Biomedical
Research Association (CBRA), among
others. The AMA argues that "research

> Cite sources
> parenthetically
> in text

> Provide
> closure for
> paragraphs

> Place familiar
> abbreviations
> of
> organizations
> in parentheses
> after first
> citation of
> name

6

involving animals is absolutely essential to maintaining and improving the
health of the American people" (67),
and the CBRA cites these advancements
as evidence: immunizations for polio,
diphtheria, mumps, measles and
hepatitis; treatments such as antibiotics, insulin, antiinflammation medicine, chemotherapy, and surgeries such
as coronary bypass, replacement of
joints, reattachment of severed limbs,
and heart, lung, kidney and liver
transplants (n. pag.). The AMA supports the CBRA's claims.

Despite these assertions, opposition to vivisection includes people
from all occupations and social divi-
sions. The AAVS counts Mark Twain,
Abraham Lincoln, Gandhi, Henry Salt,
George Bernard Shaw, and composer
Richard Wagner as vocal protesters to
experiments on animals (Health and
Humane 6). In addition, one could
cite many others, such as Nobel
laureate Isaac Beshevis Singer and

Use paraphrase to summarize source's content

Use short title for discussing work

Cite both title and page numbers to distinguish several works by same author

7

theologian C. S. Lewis. Indeed, some
researchers, like Michael A. Fox, who
once supported animal experimentation,
now vociferously oppose it.[2] Many
physicians disagree with the AMA's
stance on vivisection and have created
the Physicians Committee for Responsible Medicine (PCRM). According to
the PCRM, research on animals is highly
unreliable:

> Many animal experiments produce
> results that are far from relevant
> to human health. . . . Animals and
> humans differ in medically impor-
> tant ways, and often animal experi-
> ments can produce misleading
> results. . . .(n. pag.)

Clearly, the PCRM's criticism is anti-
thetical to the claims of the CBRA, and
this disagreement is the basis for the
battle between the two groups.

During the past thirty years,
protests against the use and/or misuse
of laboratory animals have become more
numerous and vocal. In the 1960s, the
increase in the number of animals used

Use colon to introduce long quotation

Indent long quotations 10 spaces from left margin; double-space all such blocked quotations

Cite source for long, indented quotation at the end, following final period

8

for research elicited public concern
and prompted legislation to initiate
the Animal Welfare Act of 1966. Since
the 1970s, new animal protection agencies have rejuvenated the older welfare movements. In fact, many people
who formerly supported the reform of
the animal experimentation system have
begun to argue more strongly for the
abolition of the whole system. Polls
of the general public also show an
increasing awareness of the problems
involved in using animals for experimentation. For example, James M.
Jasper and Dorothy Nelkin estimate
that ten to fifteen million Americans
now donate funds to animal rights
agencies (3), and this estimate illustrates the magnitude of the prevailing
controversy. Groups such as PETA and
the AAVS are but two of the seven
thousand animal protection groups now
present in the United States.
According to Burroughs Wellcome, a
pharmaceutical company, these groups

9

claim a membership of over ten million people with a budget of over fifty million dollars.

Admittedly, some protests have been more extreme. Abolitionists, for example, took drastic measures to gain the public eye and raise public aware-ness on the issue of animal experimen-tation. According to Jeffrey L. Fox, on Memorial Day 1984 five members of the Animal Liberation Front (ALF) entered the vacant head-injury laboratory at the University of Pennsylvania Medical School and ruined over twenty-thousand dollars' worth of laboratory equipment. The group also stole video tapes that the laboratory had created while filming some of its experiments (1319). According to Peter Singer in Animal Liberation, when the tapes were viewed, they were seen to contain footage of "conscious, unanesthetized baboons struggling as they were being strapped down before the head injuries were inflicted" (81). The video tapes were

10

publicized by the PETA organization, and the funding for the head-injury experiments was later stopped. ALF has made over a hundred more such raids and such attacks have resulted in considerable publicity, both positive and negative, for animal rights activists.

Polls of the general public also show an increasing awareness of the problems involved in using animals for experimentation. A Gallup organization survey of June 1987 indicated that 77 percent of 1,500 adults polled agreed that "the use of animals in biomedical research is necessary for medical progress." The survey indicated that only 17 percent disagreed, and 6 percent were unsure (qtd. in Burroughs Wellcome). However, in a more recent survey conducted at Eastern Kentucky University, only 52 of the 100 respondents indicated that they agreed with the statement, and 38 percent, a much larger percentage than the Gallup poll showed, said they were unsure. While

Use *qtd. in* to indicate indirect source

Provide editorial comment on outside information

11

these surveys cannot be used to determine which of the arguments is correct,
they do demonstrate that the public
concern about the usefulness of animal
research is growing.

Researchers, too, are becoming
increasingly aware of the public's concern. From a meeting of the Research
Defense Society recently held in
London, Gail Vines reported that scientists feel that they must educate the
public about the human benefits of
animal research (10). This is a huge
understatement. If the public were to
become better informed about the benefits and liabilities of such research,
the education gained would only serve
to prove that animal rights activists
and those who oppose vivisection have
by far the better argument. The use of
animals in biomedical research often
does not benefit human health and often
delays medical advancement.

Of paramount importance are the
physiological differences between human

Thesis repeated
after back-
ground section

Lines of
arguments
begin here

12

animals and nonhuman animals. These dissimilarities negate most findings or throw their validity into question. For instance, according to Paul Binding, "Penicillin kills guinea-pigs but cures humans; belladonna kills humans but is acceptable to rabbits; morphine sends humans to sleep, but induces hyperactivity in cats" (22). With so many differences in reactions to drugs, tests on animals can be either worthless or dangerous because they provide a false sense of security that the reactions in humans will be similar.

Animals' physiological systems, though superficially comparable to those of a human being, differ in subtle ways that are not always easily understood by researchers. Roy Kupsinel, a practicing physician and former president of the Tuberculosis and Respiratory Disease Association, contends that the differences between species make drug testing using animals highly unreli-

able. Kupsinel categorizes five basic
stages of action that a drug takes in a
living organism: absorption into the
bloodstream, distribution to the site
of action, mechanism of action, metabo-
lism, and elimination. In any of the
five stages, significant differences in
reactions between species may be
observed (4). Though many physicians
still advocate the use of animals for
drug testing, Kupsinel's views are held
by an increasing number of researchers
and practitioners who also believe that
animal tests are an inadequate method
of testing.

The potential danger of using animals as subjects in drug and product
testing is exemplified by the number of
approved drugs and products that are
later withdrawn. In <u>Health and Humane
Research</u>, the AAVS reports that "51.5
percent of 198 drugs approved by the FDA
between 1976 and 1985 caused severe
adverse reactions after they were marketed" (10). The animal testing per-

14

formed on these drugs gave no indication
of adverse reactions, and these drugs
were later withdrawn. The following are
examples of those drugs that gave no
indication in animals that there would
be adverse reactions in humans:

Drug (Purpose)	Brand Name	Launched	Withdrawn
Ticrynafen (diuretic)	Selacryn	1979	1980
Benoxaprofen (analgesic)	Oraflex	1982	1982
Zomepirac (analgesic)	Zomax	1980	1983
Nomifensine (antidepressant)	Merital	1984	1986
Suprofen (analgesic)	Suprol	1985	1987 (11)

The longest that any of these drugs
remained on the market was about three
years. When researchers had gathered
sufficient information from the human
consumption of these drugs, the medications were withdrawn. Consequently,
human reactions to medications are not
really known until the medications are
tested on humans themselves. Ulti-

Explain graphs
and charts

15

mately, human beings are now and have always been the real guinea pigs.

We are able to see the drawbacks of drug testing using animals when we take a closer look at the history of some drugs that were later withdrawn. Perhaps the most well known example of an animal-tested drug that had tragic human consequences was the drug thalidomide. Thalidomide was a drug initially marketed as a sedative and tested safe for laboratory rats, dogs, cats, hamsters, and chickens. But as Peter Singer informs us, thalidomide ultimately caused severe birth defects in over 10,000 children. Singer also reminds us that it was the physiological differences between human animals and nonhuman animals that caused researchers to overlook potential hazards (57).

Cancer research using animals is notorious for its unreliability. Philip Abelson reports that the principal method of determining potential carcinogens is based on experiments in

Place author's name in the text to introduce outside information

16

which animals are forced to ingest huge
quantities of a substance over a period
of time--usually the length of the animals' lives. Foods such as "apples,
bananas, carrots, celery, coffee, let-
tuce, orange juice, peas, potatoes, and
tomatoes" were all found to cause
cancer in laboratory rodents (1357)--
strange, because it has long been known
that human diets rich in fruits and
vegetables reduce the incidence of
human cancers.

The failure of animal research to
produce valid results in the battle for
human health does not end with carcino-
genic identification. Also in question
is the validity of experiments that
create animal models by artificially
inducing illnesses in healthy animals.
Again, the differences between human
animals and nonhuman animals demonstrate that such research is considerably questionable, if not worthless.

A major difficulty researchers
encounter is that of creating suitable

17

animal models for diseases that imitate
illnesses in human beings. This
process often takes years. Even after
a suitable animal model has been created, the diseases more often than not
fail to mirror the so-called comparable
diseases in humans. According to the
AAVS, researchers commonly create
animal models by implanting the genes
of human beings into other species.
The AAVS contends that this kind of
research is "highly unreliable" and
that such research "leads to unpre-
dictable results" ("What's Behind" 2).
With the physical differences between
human animals and nonhuman animals in
mind, it is easy to understand why the
AAVS objects to animal research.

The sentiments of the AAVS are also
supported by the editors of <u>Lancet</u>, a
British medical journal, who also affirm
that research obtained with such
artificially induced disease might be
expected to have little relation to
human disease because of the many dis-

18

similarities between rodents and human
beings (qtd. in Sharpe 76). A large
number of physicians and researchers
agree that human diseases and human
illnesses must be studied in the clinical setting--that is, they must be
studied in humans, where the diseases
naturally and spontaneously occur. The
study of artificially induced disease in
animals is of little relevance and
serves only to waste time and funding.

Use transitional signals to mark move-ment of ideas

Another problem that the use of
animal research gives rise to is that
it delays the availability of beneficial
medications and medical procedures to
Americans because federal law requires
that medical drugs and procedures be
thoroughly tested in the United States.
As Edward F. Dolan, Jr. reports, "U.S.
regulations do not recognize the evaluations made by other nations" (43)--
therefore, consumers must wait for our
own required animal tests to confirm the
use of the medication. If more reliable and quicker methods of testing

were employed, new drugs would reach
the patients much sooner and with more
information about benefits and side
effects.

An additional drawback is that the
cost of animal research is enormous
when it is compared with more reliable
techniques. According to PETA, con-
sumer product testing using animals
costs around $400,000 per product,
whereas tests using alternative methods
cost just one tenth that (<u>Alternatives</u>
2). PETA further reports that the NIH
alone dispenses upwards of $5 billion a
year to research performed on animals
(<u>Animal Experimentation</u>). Given the
hundreds of other sources of funding
for animal research, the cost to the
taxpayers is assuredly an astonishing
waste of funds.

The funding dumped into such use-
less research could better benefit the
health of all species if it were
applied to the development of more
credible research techniques. Monique

20

Winther, board member of the Lexington
Humane Society in Kentucky, agrees when
she says that experimentation on animal
models is "often duplicative and
wasteful of resources." However, the
real cost of animal research cannot be
measured, for it is the cost of life.
We will never know just how many human
and nonhuman lives can be preserved
unless we pursue alternative means of
biomedical research with more vigor.
Until then, animal research will serve
only as a deterrent to medical
progress.

    Despite the obvious drawbacks of
animal research, some people maintain
that the cost of a few animals' lives
is a small price to pay for the medical
advances and preservation of human
life. Further, they assert that
without animal experimentation there
would be no medical progress. Robert
J. White is one such individual who
asserts that "there is virtually no
major treatment or surgical procedure

**Refutation
begins here**

in modern medicine that could have been developed without animal research" (127). White erroneously contends that almost all medical progress has been achieved through vivisection. In addition, White even credits animal experimentation with discoveries leading to the development of the cure for diabetes, the decrease in childhood deaths from measles and diphtheria, and the development of antibiotics. However, what White fails to mention is that animal research frequently serves only to prove in animals what has already been discovered through the observation of humans. Often, the failure to obtain suitable animal models for this proof delays approval of a beneficial medical technique or medication until the model is created.

For instance, experiments were implemented to discover the critical link between the pancreas and diabetes. However, the initial discovery of the crucial role of the pancreas had

22

already been achieved through the study of autopsies of patients who had died from the disease. The animal experiments were later performed only to prove the initial hypothesis. As Sydney S. Lazarus and Bruno W. Volk recount, diabetes could not even be simulated in a dog until the entire pancreas was removed. After the initial findings of the researchers who studied human diabetes, the animal model was used only to prove the relationship between the pancreas and diabetes (2).

While vivisectionists would like to take credit for the reduction of childhood illness and the increase of the human life expectancy, statistical evidence demonstrates that factors such as a decline in poverty, overcrowding, and the improvement of many socioeconomic circumstances contributed far more to the eradication of human disease than did results obtained through animal research. Edward H. Kass, president of the Infectious Diseases Society of

Use rhetorically accurate verbs when introducing outside information

23

America, reports that the number of
deaths due to diphtheria, scarlet
fever, measles, tuberculosis and
whooping cough, as well as many others,
was already declining in an "almost
linear fashion" before the introduction
of vaccines, and the treatments did
little to affect the overall decline in
illnesses (111-113). With Kass's
statement in mind, it is clear that
animal research did not make the
significant impact on the decline of
childhood disease that vivisectionists
claim it did.

The discovery of antibiotics was
also not achieved through animal
research, but by a combination of human
clinical studies and in vitro experiments. According to Boris Sokoloff,
the real clues to the nature of antibiotics were produced by Dr. F.
d'Hérelle, who discovered the link
between vaccine and dysentery by
studying human patients with the disease (29). Like many of the claims of

24

those who support animal research, the
credit for the discovery of antibiotics
goes not to the vivisectionists, but to
those who conducted clinical studies on
human patients.

Many medical achievements have, of
course, been produced through animal
research. Because it continues to be
the primary means of biomedical
research in the United States, and
because massive amounts of funding are
allotted to such experimentation, by
odds alone, such research must have
achieved something.

However, the point is that those
who support animal research continue to
exaggerate its importance by convincing
the public that without vivisection
medical progress would grind to a halt.
The PCRM reminds us that clinical
studies, not animal research, have produced the most significant medical
advances in the research of cancer,
heart disease, stroke, trauma, and respiratory disease, all of which are the

primary threats to human health today
(n. pag.). In light of these advances,
it becomes clear that if vivisection
were eliminated tomorrow, medical
progress would not only continue, but
would surge forward with an unequaled
swiftness because of added investment
in--and research for--more reliable
research techniques.

Another contention generated by
those who support animal research is
that there are no viable alternatives.
Further, many suggest that the abolition of animal research would necessi-
tate experimentation on humans.
Neither of these statements could be
further from the truth.

As noted earlier, many alternatives
for toxicity and drug testing exist.
As Alan M. Goldberg and John M. Frazier
report, the Center for Alternatives to
Animal Testing at Johns Hopkins University has determined that there are over
thirty alternative in vitro tests to
replace toxicity and drug testing using

26

animals (28). Many of these tests
expose tissue cultures of human cells
or embryos to the chemical being
studied. Such tests are less expensive
and have more validity than those using
animals. Not only does the use of in
vitro testing save many animals from
suffering, but it also saves consumers
and taxpayers millions of dollars.

The focus on prevention, rather
than on treatment, is another alternative to animal research. While a few
people may benefit from the advances
that vivisection produces, many others
die for the lack of basic health treatment and education. World Medicine
found that 78 percent of all human cancers are preventable or due to environmental factors (qtd. in AAVS Health and
Humane 8), and the number one threat to
human health, heart disease, can usually be prevented by a change of diet
and lifestyle. According to Paul
Binding, however, only 1 percent of
medical research funding is allocated

27

to prevention of disease (22). If the
money now squandered on irrelevant
animal studies were applied to disease
prevention, human health would certainly benefit.

Recently developed synthetic human
models can be used as substitutes for
animals in educational settings. Medical students can practice on human
cadavers and use computer simulations.
Some universities in the United States
and England now train medical students
without using animals. If these universities can successfully produce
qualified graduates, then the question
of whether animals are needed in education has certainly been answered.

Given the irrelevancy of animal
research, it is not surprising to learn
that clinical studies of human beings
have been, and will continue to be, the
most valuable research tool. As Robert
Sharpe asserts, "clinical studies must
still be carried out if the disease is
to be properly understood: doctors can

28

only hope that animal models do not confuse their clinical findings" (173). Willing human volunteers, suffering from disease, are often denied experimental treatments because of the false assumption that medical treatments and drugs must first be tried and proven effective in animal models. Clinical study is the most obvious and effective method of conducting biomedical research, and it is the study of humans and human disease that will serve to advance our knowledge far beyond what has been achieved through animal research.

If animal experimentation is such a faulty method of research, then why does it continue? Another part of the answer lies in the inertia of the medical community. Yet the researchers themselves cannot become our scapegoats. The use of animals for the purposes of our own species has also been, since the beginning of time, an integral part of human society. Many sci-

29

entists are systematically desensitized
throughout their lives and by the
process of education to the suffering
they inflict.

Conclusion
begins here

Fortunately, today many organizations such as PETA and the AAVS pub-
licly oppose vivisection and have
achieved unprecedented short-term gains
in the abolition of such wasteful
research. However, an end to animal
research must begin with a change in
our own attitudes toward other species.
We must grant other species the same
consideration that we grant our own and
teach our children to do the same. We
must ensure that the human species does
not profit from the exploitation and
suffering of other species. This
reshaping of our own perspectives may
take decades or even centuries to complete, but only through the fulfillment
of such aspirations can we preserve our
own morality, and quite possibly our
own future.

30

Notes

1. I wish to thank the members of my research group--Jeremy Banks, Lea Kell, Kathisha Seward, and Dana Singleton--for their assistance while I worked on this research project. I especially appreciate their willingness to share information with me and the editorial help they provided.

2. The story of Michael A. Fox is interesting. In 1986 he published <u>The Case for Animal Experimentation</u>, a book that was well received by many researchers. To everyone's surprise, however, within a year Fox completely changed his mind. Radically disagreeing with the arguments presented in his book, Fox now writes to explain why he no longer believes in animal experimentation. Those who wish to read Fox's explanation for his reversal will want to examine "Animal Experimentation: A Philosopher's Changing Views," "Animal Research Reconsidered: A Former Defender of Vivisection

Place content notes after the text and before Works Cited

Title the list of notes *Notes*

31

Struggles with His Radical Change of
Heart," and "The Philosopher Who Came
in from the Cold: Interview with
Michael Fox by Marly Cornell."

32

Works Cited

Abelson, Philip. "Testing for Carcinogens with Rodents." Science 249
(21 Sep. 1991): 1357.

American Anti-Vivisection Society
(AAVS). Health and Humane
Research. Jenkintown, PA: AAVS,
n.d.

---. Vivisection. It's Shocking.
AAVS, n.d.

---. "What's Behind the Patenting of
Animals?" The AV (2 July 1992): 2.

American Medical Association (AMA).
"Animal Experimentation Benefits
Human Health." Rohr 59-67.

Binding, Paul. "Prisoners of Science."
New Statesman & Society (13 Dec.
1991): 21-22.

Burroughs Wellcome Company. Wellcome
News. n.d.

California Biomedical Research Association (CBRA). Health Research to
Benefit People and Animals. n.d.

Dolan, Edward F., Jr. Animal Rights.
New York: Dolan, 1986.

Title the
reference list
Works Cited

Alphabetize
entries by
authors' last
names

Cross-reference
articles from
Opposing
Viewpoints
anthologies

35

Fox, Jeffrey L. "Lab Break-in Stirs
    Animal Welfare Debate." Science 224
    (22 June 1984): 1319-20.
Fox, Michael A. "Animal Experimenta-
    tion: A Philosopher's Changing
    Views." Between the Species 3
    (1987): 55-60, 75, 80, 82.
---. "Animal Research Reconsidered: A
    Former Defender of Vivisection
    Struggles with His Radical Change
    of Heart." New Age Journal
    (Jan./Feb. 1988): 14-15, 18,21.
---. The Case for Animal Experimenta-
    tion. Berkeley, CA: U California
    P, 1986.
---. "The Philosopher Who Came in from
    the Cold: Interview with Michael
    Fox by Marly Cornell." Animals'
    Agenda 8 (Mar. 1988): 7-10.
Goldberg, Alan M., and John M. Frazier.
    "Alternatives to Animals in Toxi-
    city Testing." Scientific American
    261 (Aug. 1989): 24-30.

Use three
unspaced
hyphens to
represent
author's name
when multiple
works listed by
same author

34

Jasper, James M., and Dorothy Nelkin.
   The Animal Rights Crusade: The
   Growth of a Moral Protest.   New
   York: Free, 1992.

Kass, Edward H.   "Infectious Disease
   and Social Change." Journal of
   Infectious Diseases 123 (Jan.
   1971): 110-14.

Kupsinel, Roy.   Vivisection: Science or
   Sham.   People for Reason in Science
   and Medicine, 1990.

Lazarus, Sydney S., and Bruno W. Volk.
   The Pancreas in Human and Experimental Diabetes.   New York: Grune
   and Stratton, 1962.

People for the Ethical Treatment of
   Animals (PETA).   Alternatives:
   Testing without Torture.   Factsheet
   #11.   n.d.

---.   Animal Experimentation: Sadistic
   Scandal.   Factsheet #1.   n.d.

---.   LD-50 Tests: Lethal Tests.   Factsheet #9.   n.d.

35

Physicians Committee for Responsible
 Medicine (PCRM). The Facts About
 Animal Experimentation. n.d.

Rohr, Janelle, ed. Animal Rights:
 Opposing Viewpoints. San Diego,
 CA: Greenhaven, 1989.

Sharpe, Robert. The Cruel Deception.
 Northamptonshire, Wellingborough,
 England: Thorsons, 1988.

Singer, Peter. Animal Liberation. New
 York: Avon, 1990.

Sokoloff, Boris. The Miracle Drugs.
 New York: Ziff-Davis, 1949.

Vines, Gail. "Researchers Rally Behind
 Animal Experiments." New Scientist
 130 (4 May 1991): 10.

Westacott, E. A Century of Vivisection
 and Antivivisection. Ashington,
 England: Daniel, 1949.

White, Robert J. "The Facts About
 Animal Research." Reader's Digest
 (Mar. 1988): 127-32.

Winther, Monique. Interview by Susan
 Mattingly. 5 Nov. 1992.

Use editor's name for books in Opposing Viewpoints series

Form for personal interview

APPENDIX B

Evaluation Guides

To indicate how well you are doing and what improvements you can make, use the evaluation guides that have been prepared for the suggested writing assignments. These guides give you a template to use when thinking and talking about individual assignments. By looking at an evaluation guide carefully, you can see what your instructor may expect. You can also use them as checklists to determine how well, in your estimation, you have satisfied suggested writing tasks. Inasmuch as these evaluation guides may accompany graded assignments through several revisions, they also serve as indicators to help you find the direction in which your improvements might lead. Finally, these evaluation guides give your instructor an opportunity to mark the quality of your work with a grade or perhaps a grade in progress.

Your instructor may ask you to photocopy these evaluation guides so that they may be attached to writing assignments.

Name _____ Class _____ Date _____

Précis Number _____ Draft Number _____

Evaluation Guide for Suggested Writing Assignment 1
Write a Rhetorical Précis on One or More Essays

I. The first sentence provides the following information:
- the name of the author
- title of the essay or article
- (date and additional publishing information in parentheses)
- a rhetorically accurate verb and a "that" clause containing the major assertion (thesis) of the work

1   2   3   4   5

II. The second sentence provides a brief but accurate explanation describing how the author develops or supports the central idea (thesis) of the essay; this information is most likely given in the same order as it is developed in the essay; to convey such information, several independent clauses may be linked with semicolons (just as this single sentence is made up of three independent clauses linked together with semicolons).

1   2   3   4   5

III. The third sentence describes the author's purpose and does so by using an "in order to" phrase.

1   2   3   4   5

IV. The fourth sentence provides the reader with a good description of the intended audience and describes the relationship that the author establishes with the audience.

1   2   3   4   5

V. Readers comprehend the précis easily because the writer has full command of sentence structure, punctuation, and spelling.

1   2   3   4   5

(Your instructor may ask you to photocopy this evaluation guide and attach it to the writing assignment.)

Name_____ Class_____ Date_____

Draft Number _____

Evaluation Guide for Suggested Writing Assignment 2
Make Dialectical Notes on One or More Essays

I. These dialectical notes are properly set up; that is, they are arranged in two columns. One column contains numbered note entries reflecting the contents of the paragraphs; another column contains commentary on those notes.

1   2   3   4   5

II. The notes reflect critical reading and mature responses.

1   2   3   4   5

(Your instructor may ask you to photocopy this evaluation guide and attach it to the writing assignment.)

Name_____ Class_____ Date_____

Draft Number _____

Evaluation Guide for Suggested Writing Assignment 3
Make a Charted Reading of One or More Essays

I. This charted reading is properly set up; that is, it provides numbered boxes for notes on all corresponding numbered paragraphs; in each box are notes restating the content of each paragraph.

1   2   3   4   5

II. The notes reflect critical reading and mature responses.

1   2   3   4   5

(Your instructor may ask you to photocopy this evaluation guide and attach it to the writing assignment.)

Name_____ Class_____ Date_____

Draft Number _____

Evaluation Guide for Suggested Writing Assignment 4
Write to Several Organizations for Information

I. The business letters follow the form generally used for such correspondence.

1   2   3   4   5

II. Readers comprehend the requests made in these letters easily because the writer has full command of sentence structure, punctuation, and spelling.

1   2   3   4   5

(Your instructor may ask you to photocopy this evaluation guide and attach it to the writing assignment.)

Name _____ Class_____ Date _____

Draft Number _____

Evaluation Guide for Suggested Writing Assignments 5-15
Develop Background Information (Chapter 2)
Use the MLA Documentation Style (Chapter 3)

Incorporating one or more strategies for developing a background report, this piece of writing demonstrates the following skills:

I. The writer knows how to report important background information by composing paragraphs that are controlled by a topic sentence.

1   2   3   4   5

II. Information within the paragraphs supports topic sentences. That is, each sentence within a paragraph explains, clarifies, develops, or lends support to the topic sentence. The paragraphs are logically and coherently developed.

1   2   3   4   5

III. Outside sources incorporated into the paragraph are properly introduced.

1   2   3   4   5

IV. Outside source material is either quoted exactly, paraphrased adequately, or summarized fairly.

1   2   3   4   5

V. An editorial "coming-away" comment follows the use of outside information.

1   2   3   4   5

VI. Each paragraph is rounded off with appropriate closure.

1   2   3   4   5

VII. The writer provides a works cited entry for each citation of outside source material.

1   2   3   4   5

(Your instructor may ask you to photocopy this evaluation guide and attach copies to several writing assignments.)

Name_____   Class_____ Date_____

Draft Number _____

Evaluation Guide for Suggested Writing Assignment 16
Write Your Background Section

I.   The writer provides ample and extensive background information, using many of the strategies that help readers understand the topic's context.

1   2   3   4   5

II. This section demonstrates that the writer knows how to use the MLA style of documentation. The reader easily follows the presentation of material from outside sources. At least three different sources are used with the following three-step method:

A. Use of introductory tag or formal introduction for any quotation, paraphrase, or summary of data or information.
B. Exact citation, good paraphrase, or adequate summary of secondary material.
C. Inclusion of an editorial comment after use of an outside source in order to help the reader negotiate the text.

The Works Cited listing is accurate. Photocopies of outside sources are appended.

1   2   3   4   5

III. The reader comfortably follows the presentation of ideas and information because the writing is clear, thoughtful, and well organized; support is vivid, specific, and insightful; sentence structure is graceful and varied, supporting the writing's purpose with effective organizational signals; word choice is precise.

1   2   3   4   5

IV. Readers comprehend this section easily because the writer has full command of sentence structure, punctuation, and spelling.

1   2   3   4   5

(Your instructor may ask you to photocopy this evaluation guide and attach it to the writing assignment.)

Name _____ Class_____ Date_____

Draft Number _____

Evaluation Guide for Suggested Writing Assignment 17
Compose a Tentative Works Cited List

I. The Works Cited contains at least six entries; it meets all of the general format requirements:
   - It is double-spaced consistently throughout.
   - The list is arranged alphabetically by authors' last names.
   - The title of the page (Works Cited) is centered; it is neither underlined nor in quotation marks.
   - The first line of each entry is flush left; all other lines of an entry are indented.

1   2   3   4   5

II. Entries in Works Cited are accurately modeled after examples for books, articles in periodicals, and other sources. The entries are accurate in their presentation of bibliographic details.

1   2   3   4   5

III. Readers understand and use the listing easily because the writer has full command of punctuation and spelling.

1   2   3   4   5

(Your instructor may ask you to photocopy this evaluation guide and attach it to the writing assignment.)

Name_____ Class_____ Date_____

Draft Number _____

Evaluation Guide for Suggested Writing Assignment 18
Write a Thesis That You Will Support

I.   The thesis focuses on a single issue.

1   2   3   4   5

II.   The thesis is appropriate for a research paper.

1   2   3   4   5

III. The thesis indicates how the central idea will be developed.

1   2   3   4   5

IV.   Readers comprehend the thesis easily because the writer has full command of its sentence structure, punctuation, and spelling.

1   2   3   4   5

(Your instructor may ask you to photocopy this evaluation guide and attach it to the writing assignment.)

Name _____ Class_____ Date_____

Draft Number _____

Evaluation Guide for Suggested Writing Assignment 19
Work Out the Structure for Your Research Paper

   I.   The writer provides a tentative title for this writing.

1   2   3   4   5

  II.   The writer provides a thoughtful thesis statement (based on critical reading and research) that clearly governs the structure of this writing.

1   2   3   4   5

 III.   The writer provides a proposed outline that lists and details the contents of this writing; this outline follows the conventions of outlining in that the descending parts are labels in appropriate order.

1   2   3   4   5

 IV.   The writer presents an outline that contains substantial and intelligent support for the thesis.

1   2   3   4   5

  V.   Readers comprehend the outline easily. If a sentence outline has been required, the writer has full command of sentence structure, punctuation, and spelling.

1   2   3   4   5

(Your instructor may ask you to photocopy this evaluation guide and attach it to the writing assignment.)

Name_____ Class_____ Date_____

Draft Number _____

Evaluation Guide for Suggested Writing Assignment 20
Write the Lines-of-Argument Section

I.   The writer supports the thesis with a number of arguments that are logical, well developed, and persuasive.

1   2   3   4   5

II. This section demonstrates that the writer knows how to use the MLA style of documentation. The reader easily follows the presentation of material from outside sources. At least three different sources are used with the following three-step method:

A. Use of introductory tag or formal introduction for any quotation, paraphrase, or summary of data or information.
B. Exact citation, good paraphrase, or adequate summary of secondary material.
C. Inclusion of an editorial comment after use of an outside source in order to help the reader negotiate the text.

The Works Cited listing is accurate. Photocopies of outside sources are appended.

1   2   3   4   5

III. The reader comfortably follows the presentation of ideas and information because the writing is clear, thoughtful, and well organized; support is vivid, specific, and insightful; sentence structure is graceful and varied, supporting the writing's purpose with effective organizational signals; word choice is precise.

1   2   3   4   5

IV. Readers comprehend this section easily because the writer has full command of sentence structure, punctuation, and spelling.

1   2   3   4   5

(Your instructor may ask you to photocopy this evaluation guide and attach it to the writing assignment.)

Name _____ Class _____ Date _____

Draft Number _____

Evaluation Guide for Suggested Writing Assignment 21
Write the Refutation or Reconciliation

I. The writer provides several well-developed opposing arguments that are effectively refuted. These arguments are convincingly refuted because the writer has provided counterarguments, or the writer effectively reconciles opposing viewpoints by proposing some sort of compromise, negotiation, or reconciliation. Significant research has been incorporated into this section of the paper.

1   2   3   4   5

II. This section demonstrates that the writer knows how to use the MLA style of documentation. The reader easily follows the presentation of material from outside sources. At least three different sources are used with the following three-step method:

A. Use of introductory tag or formal introduction for any quotation, paraphrase, or summary of data or information.
B. Exact citation, good paraphrase, or adequate summary of secondary material.
C. Inclusion of an editorial comment after use of an outside source in order to help the reader negotiate the text.

The Works Cited listing is accurate. Photocopies of outside sources are appended.

1   2   3   4   5

III. The reader comfortably follows the presentation of ideas and information because the writing is clear, thoughtful, and well organized; support is vivid, specific, and insightful; sentence structure is graceful and varied, supporting the writing's purpose with effective organizational signals; word choice is precise.

1   2   3   4   5

IV. Readers comprehend this section easily because the writer has full command of sentence structure, punctuation, and spelling.

1   2   3   4   5

(Your instructor may ask you to photocopy this evaluation guide and attach it to the writing assignment.)

Name_____ Class_____ Date_____

Draft Number _____

Evaluation Guide for Suggested Writing Assignment 22
Create a Title and Write the Introduction

I. The choice of title is appropriate to the essay. It makes a strong first impression; it can be trusted; it is easily understood; it is interesting.

1   2   3   4   5

II. If the introduction makes use of source material, it demonstrates that the writer knows how to use the MLA style of documentation. The reader easily follows the presentation of material from outside sources. At least three different sources are used with the following three-step method:

A. Use of introductory tag or formal introduction for any quotation, paraphrase, or summary of data or information.
B. Exact citation, good paraphrase, or adequate summary of secondary material.
C. Inclusion of an editorial comment after use of an outside source in order to help the reader negotiate the text.

The Works Cited listing is accurate. Photocopies of outside sources are appended.

1   2   3   4   5

III. The reader comfortably follows the presentation of ideas and information because the writing is clear, thoughtful, and well organized; support is vivid, specific, and insightful; sentence structure is graceful and varied, supporting the writing's purpose with effective organizational signals; word choice is precise.

1   2   3   4   5

IV. Readers comprehend this section easily because the writer has full command of sentence structure, punctuation, and spelling.

1   2   3   4   5

(Your instructor may ask you to photocopy this evaluation guide and attach it to the writing assignment.)

Name_____ Class_____ Date_____

Draft Number _____

Evaluation Guide for Suggested Writing Assignment 23
Write the Conclusion

I. The conclusion provides satisfactory closure for the whole essay. While it sums up the essay, it also gives the reader an opportunity to think about its implications, or it suggests activities that the reader might promote.

1   2   3   4   5

II. If the conclusion makes use of source material, it demonstrates that the writer knows how to use the MLA style of documentation. The reader easily follows the presentation of material from outside sources. At least three different sources are used with the following three-step method:

A. Use of introductory tag or formal introduction for any quotation, paraphrase, or summary of data or information.
B. Exact citation, good paraphrase, or adequate summary of secondary material.
C. Inclusion of an editorial comment after use of an outside source in order to help the reader negotiate the text.

The Works Cited listing is accurate. Photocopies of outside sources are appended.

1   2   3   4   5

III. The reader comfortably follows the presentation of ideas and information because the writing is clear, thoughtful, and well organized; support is vivid, specific, and insightful; sentence structure is graceful and varied, supporting the writing's purpose with effective organizational signals; word choice is precise.

1   2   3   4   5

IV. Readers comprehend this section easily because the writer has full command of sentence structure, punctuation, and spelling.

1   2   3   4   5

(Your instructor may ask you to photocopy this evaluation guide and attach it to the writing assignment.)

Name_____ Class_____ Date_____

Draft Number _____

Evaluation Guide for Suggested Writing Assignment 24
Prepare the Presentation Copy

I.   The presentation copy satisfies the format requirements of the MLA style for a research paper: readable print, consistent double-spacing, appropriate margins, indentations, identification of writer, title placement, pagination, and use of any tables or illustrations.

1   2   3   4   5

II. The presentation copy offers a clear, thoughtful, well-organized approach to the research topic. With a strong thesis as its foundation, the paper provides vivid, specific, and insightful support for the thesis. The paper is well organized. Paragraphs are well developed and coherent. The movement from one idea to the next is logical. The sentence structure is graceful and varied, supporting the paper's purpose through effective organizational signals. Word choice is precise.

1   2   3   4   5

III. The presentation copy demonstrates that the writer knows how to use the MLA style of documentation. The reader easily follows the presentation of material from outside sources. A sufficient number of sources are used with the following three-step method:

A. Use of introductory tag or formal introduction for any quotation, paraphrase, or summary of data or information.
B. Exact citation, good paraphrase, or adequate summary of secondary material.
C. Inclusion of an editorial comment after use of an outside source in order to help the reader negotiate the text.

The Works Cited listing is accurate. Photocopies of outside sources are appended.

1   2   3   4   5

IV. Readers comprehend the paper easily because the writer has full command of sentence structure, punctuation, and spelling.

1   2   3   4   5

(Your instructor may ask you to photocopy this evaluation guide and attach it to the writing assignment.)

APPENDIX C

How to Prepare a Research Paper Portfolio

Your instructor may require you to develop and submit a research paper portfolio, a collection of your writings that shows the process by which you arrived at the presentation copy of your paper. Indeed, your instructor may use your portfolio to evaluate the whole of your semester's work. Inasmuch, the, as a portfolio reflects the total writing process, it should include all writing assignments, evaluation guides, all drafts and revisions of the research paper, and any source material you used during the composing process. Your instructor may also require a letter of reflection, that is, your self-evaluation of the portfolio's contents. To help your instructor review your portfolio, organize it as shown in the illustration.

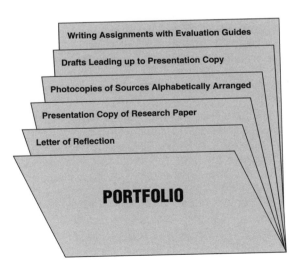

Works Cited

Adelstein, Michael E., and Jean G. Pival. *The Writing Commitment*. New York: Harcourt, 1994.

Baker, Sheridan. *The Practical Stylist*. New York: Harper, 1985.

Baugh, L. Sue. *How to Write Term Papers and Reports*. Lincolnwood, IL: VGM Career Horizons, 1993.

Beasley, David. *How to Use a Research Library*. New York: Oxford UP, 1988.

Berthoff, Ann E., with James Stephens. *Forming/Thinking/Writing*. Portsmouth, NH: Boynton/Cook, 1988.

Connors, Robert, and Cheryl Glenn. *The St. Martin's Guide to Teaching Writing*. New York: St. Martin's, 1992.

Cook, Claire Kehrwald. *Line by Line: How to Edit Your Own Writing*. Boston: Houghton Mifflin, 1985.

Corbett, Edward P. J. *Classical Rhetoric for the Modern Student*. New York: Oxford UP, 1990.

Elbow, Peter, and Pat Belanoff. *A Community of Writers: A Workshop Course in Writing*. New York: Random House, 1989.

Gibaldi, Joseph, and Walter S. Achtert. *MLA Handbook for Writers of Research Papers*. New York: Modern Language Association, 1988.

Horner, Winifred Bryan. *Rhetoric in the Classical Tradition*. New York: St. Martin's, 1988.

Kister, Kenneth F. *Best Encyclopedias: A Guide to General and Specialized Encyclopedias*. Phoenix, AZ: Oryx Press, 1986.

Laib, Nevin K. *Rhetoric and Style: Strategies for Advanced Writers*. Englewood Cliffs, NJ: Prentice-Hall, 1984.

Leahy, Richard. "Twenty Titles for the Writer." *College Composition and Communication* 43:4 (Dec. 1992): 516–19.

Lunsford, Andrea, and Robert Connors. *The St. Martin's Handbook*. New York: St. Martin's, 1992.

Mulford, Carolyn. "Assess Your Own Writing with Six Objective Measurements and a Breath Test." *Writing Concepts: The Newsletter of Writing and Editing* 4:1 (Jan. 1994): 1–2.

Paul, Richard W. *Critical Thinking: What Every Person Needs to Survive in a Rapidly Changing World*. Ed. A.J.A. Binker. Santa Rosa, CA: Foundation for Critical Thinking, 1992.

Perdue, Virginia. "Authority and the Freshman Writer: The Ideology of the Thesis Statement." *The Writing Instructor* 11 (Spring/Summer 1992): 135–42.

Reinking, James A., et al. *Strategies for Successful Writing: A Rhetoric and Reader*. Englewood Cliffs,NJ: Prentice-Hall, 1993.

Rohr, Janelle, ed. *Animal Rights: Opposing Viewpoints*. San Diego, CA: Greenhaven, 1989.

Singer, Peter. *Animal Liberation*. New York: Avon, 1992.

Valiukenas, Delija J. *Writing with Authority: A Guide to the Research Process*. New York: Random House, 1987.

Woodworth, Margaret K. "The Rhetorical Précis." *Rhetoric Review* 7:1 (Fall 1988): 156–63.

Index

About the Author

A ndrew Harnack is a professor of English at Eastern Kentucky University. He teaches composition courses at all levels, from freshman to advanced, as well as history of rhetoric and theories of composition. His publications include numerous articles on Renaissance literature, especially seventeenth-century poets. He has served as executive secretary and president for the Kentucky Philological Association. Having received his university's Excellence in Teaching Award, Professor Harnack is currently EKU's Writing Program administrator.